Birds of Florida

Field Guide

Second Edition

by Stan Tekiela

Adventure Publications, Inc.
Cambridge, Minnesota

...ny wife Katherine and daughter Abigail with all my love

...knowledgments

...pecial thanks to the National Wildlife Refuge System, which stewards the land that is ...critical to many bird species. Thanks also to Bill Pranty, Audubon of Florida, and Wes Biggs, President of Florida Nature Tours, for reviewing the range maps.

Edited by Sandy Livoti

Book design and illustrations by Jonathan Norberg

Range maps produced by Anthony Hertzel

Photo credits by photographer and page number:

Cover photo: Male Painted Bunting by Brian E. Small
Brian M. Collins: 274 **Cornell Laboratory of Ornithology**: 96 (perching) **Dudley Edmondson**: 92 (non-breeding adult, white juvenile), 112 (female), 116, 144, 150 (both), 164 (displaying), 170 (perching), 186 (both), 196 (soaring), 202 (all), 216 (breeding), 224, 248 (perching, soaring), 300 (in flight), 312 (breeding), 322 (winter male), 328 **Kevin T. Karlson**: 22 (soaring), 46, 62 (both), 128, 140 (female), 156, 218, 244, 302 (winter), 306 (breeding), 326 **Bill Marchel**: 4, 88 (male), 146, 284 **Maslowski Productions**: 32 (female), 96 (soaring), 106, 120, 204, 208, 226, 318 (chick-feeding adult), 332 **Arthur Morris**: 140 (male) **Steve Mortensen**: 36 (male), 78 **Warren Nelson**: 36 (female), 152 (female) **John Pennoyer**: 100 **Johann Schumacher/CLO***: 88 (female) **Brian E. Small**: 22 (perching), 26, 108, 126 (winter), 130, 162, 164 (breeding), 194, 206, 216 (winter), 270, 286, 288 (yellow male), 292, 304 (winter, juvenile), 306 (in flight), 312 (winter), 330 **Stan Tekiela**: 2, 6 (both), 8, 10, 12, 14, 16, 18, 20, 24 (both), 28 (all), 30 (all), 32 (male), 34 (both), 38 (both), 40, 42 (both), 44 (breeding), 48, 50, 52, 54, 56 (both), 58, 60 (both), 64 (both), 66 (both), 68 (all), 70, 72, 74, 76, 80 (both), 82 (both), 84, 86, 90, 92 (breeding, molting juvenile), 94, 98, 102, 104, 110, 112 (male), 114, 118, 122 (adult, 1 year old), 124, 126 (breeding), 132 (female, juvenile), 134, 136 (all), 138, 142, 148, 152 (male), 154, 158 (both), 160, 166 (both), 168, 172, 174, 176, 178, 180, 182, 184, 188, 190, 192 (winter), 198, 200, 210 (all), 212, 214, 220, 222, 228, 230, 232, 234, 236 (both), 238 (both), 240 (perching), 242, 246, 248 (juvenile), 250, 252, 254 (winter), 256 (soaring), 258 (both), 260 (both), 262 (all), 264 (both), 266 (both), 268 (both), 272, 276, 278, 280, 282, 288 (male), 290, 294 (male), 296 (all), 298 (in flight), 300 (perching), 302 (breeding, both in flight), 304 (breeding, in flight), 306 (winter), 308, 310 (both), 312 (juvenile), 314 (both), 316 (both), 318 (breeding, in flight), 320, 322 (male, female), 324 (male), 334 **Brian K. Wheeler**: 170 (soaring), 196 (perching), 256 (perching) **J. R. Woodward/CLO***: 240 (displaying) **Jim Zipp**: 44 (winter), 122 (Bohemian), 192 (breeding), 298 (perching), 324 (female)

*Cornell Laboratory of Ornithology

To the best of the publisher's knowledge, all photos were of live birds.

Third Printing
Copyright 2001, 2004 by Stan Tekiela
Published by Adventure Publications, Inc.
820 Cleveland St. S
Cambridge, MN 55008
1-800-678-7006
www.adventurepublications.net
All rights reserved
Printed in China
ISBN-13: 978-1-59193-105-8
ISBN-10: 1-59193-105-3

TABLE OF CONTENTS

Introduction

Sample Page 1

The Birds

WHY WATCH BIRDS IN FLORIDA?

Millions of people have discovered bird feeding. It's a simple and enjoyable way to bring the beauty of birds closer to your home. Watching the birds at your feeder and listening to them often leads to a lifetime pursuit of bird identification. The *Birds of Florida Field Guide* is for those who want to identify the common birds of Florida.

Listening to bird songs and learning about them is a wonderful way to expand your enjoyment of birds in Florida. The optional *Birds of Florida Audio CDs* contain nearly two hours of songs and calls of the birds in this book, as well as tips and mnemonics for learning the calls.

There are over 800 species of birds found in North America. In Florida alone there have been more than 480 different kinds of birds recorded through the years. That is an impressive amount of birds for a single state! These bird sightings were diligently recorded by hundreds of bird watchers and became part of the official state record. From these valuable records, I have chosen 140 of the most common and easily seen birds of Florida to include in this field guide.

Bird watching, often called birding, is the largest spectator sport in America. Its outstanding popularity in Florida is due, in part, to an unusually rich and abundant birdlife. Why are there so many birds in this state? One reason is water, both saltwater and fresh. Peninsular Florida is surrounded by water and has 1,350 miles (2,175 km) of coastline. It's home to many ocean-loving birds such as the colony-nesting Royal Tern and surf-running Sanderling. In addition to the coast, Florida has several hundred sizable lakes such as Lake Okeechobee–the third largest lake in the U.S.–thousands of freshwater and salt-water marshes, not to mention four major rivers. All of this water attracts millions of birds such as the Tricolored Heron and Roseate Spoonbill.

Climate is another reason why Florida has so many birds. The northern part of Florida is classified as humid subtropical, while southern Florida is considered tropical wet, more typical of Central America. The relative warm climate affords birds extra time to raise more than one brood per season, or to feed here unimpeded during severe winters elsewhere.

Southern Florida not only attracts people to its warm winter climate, it is also a winter home to hundreds of migratory bird species. From tiny birds, such as the Palm and Black-and-white Warblers, to the Ruddy Turnstone, an ornately colored shorebird that nests in coastal Alaska, millions of birds pack into southern Florida each winter to feed in the state's nutrient waters and fertile forests.

While water and weather are good reasons for a vast abundance of birds in Florida, keep in mind the great size of the state. Florida is the twenty-third largest state, covering approximately 59,900 square miles (155,700 sq. km), over 35 percent of which is covered with forest. Florida's forests are home to such birds as the Chuck-will's-widow, whose calls throughout the night can be heard each spring and summer.

Florida is one of the best places in North America to see a wide array of birds. Whether witnessing a nesting colony of herons and egrets in the Everglades or welcoming back the wintering shorebirds, bird watchers enjoy variety and excitement in Florida as each season turns to the next.

OBSERVE WITH A STRATEGY; TIPS FOR IDENTIFYING BIRDS

Identifying birds isn't as difficult as you might think. By simply following a few basic strategies, you can increase your chances of successfully identifying most birds you see! One of the first and easiest things to do when you see a new bird is to note its color. (Also, since this book is organized by color, you will go right to that color section to find it.)

Next, note the size of the bird. A strategy to quickly estimate size is to select a small-, medium- and large-sized bird to use for reference. For example, most people are familiar with robins. A robin, measured from tip of the bill to tip of the tail, is 10 inches (25 cm) long. Using the robin as an example of a medium-sized bird, select two other birds, one smaller and one larger. Many people use a House Sparrow, at about 6 inches (15 cm), and an American Crow, about 18 inches (45 cm). When you see a bird that you don't know, you can quickly ask yourself, "Is it smaller than a robin, but larger than a sparrow?" When you look in your field guide to help identify your bird, you'll know it is roughly between 6-10 inches (15-25 cm) long. This will help to narrow your choices.

Next, note the size, shape and color of the bill. Is it long, short, thick, thin, pointed, blunt, curved or straight? Seed-eating birds such as Northern Cardinals have bills that are thick and strong enough to crack even the toughest seeds. Birds that sip nectar such as Ruby-throated Hummingbirds need long thin bills to reach deep into flowers. Hawks and owls tear their prey with very sharp, curving bills. Sometimes, just noting the shape of the bill can help you decide if the bird is a woodpecker, finch, blackbird or bird of prey.

Next, take a look around and note the habitat in which you see the bird. Is it wading in a saltwater marsh? Walking along a riverbank or on the beach? Soaring in the sky? Is it perched high in the trees or hopping along the forest floor? Because of their preferences in diet and habitat, you'll usually see robins hopping on the ground, but not often eating the seeds at your feeder. Or you'll see a Blue Jay sitting on the branches of a tree, but not climbing headfirst down the trunk of a tree like the Brown-headed Nuthatch.

Noticing what a bird is eating will give you another clue to help you identify that bird. Feeding is a big part of any bird's life. Fully one-third of all bird activity revolves around searching for and catching food, or actually eating. While birds don't always follow all the rules of what we think they eat, you can make some general assumptions. Northern Flickers, for instance, feed upon ants and other insects, so you wouldn't expect to see them visiting a backyard feeder. Some birds such as Barn Swallows and Tree Swallows feed upon flying insects and spend hours swooping and diving to catch a meal.

Sometimes you can identify a bird by the way it perches. Body posture can help you differentiate between an American Crow and a Red-tailed Hawk. American Crows lean forward over their feet on a branch, while hawks perch in a vertical position. Look for this the next time you see a large unidentified bird in a tree.

Birds in flight are often difficult to identify, but noting the size and shape of the wing will help. A bird's wing size is in direct proportion to its body size, weight and type of flying. The shape of the wing determines if the bird flies fast and with precision, or slowly and less precisely. Birds such as House Finches, which flit around in thick tangles of branches, have short round wings. Birds that soar on warm updrafts of air, such as Turkey Vultures, have long broad wings. Barn Swallows have short pointed wings that slice through the air, propelling their swift and accurate flight.

Some birds have unique patterns of flight that aid in identification. American Goldfinches fly in a distinctive up-and-down pattern that makes it look as if they are riding a roller coaster.

While it's not easy to make these observations in the short time you often have to watch a "mystery bird," practicing these methods of identification will greatly expand your skills in birding. Also, seek the guidance of a more experienced birder who will help you improve your skills and answer questions on the spot.

Bird Songs and Calls

Another part of bird identification involves using your ears. A song or call can be enough to positively identify a bird without seeing it. If you see a bird that you don't know, the song or call can help you identify it. To learn about bird songs, calls, how they are produced, what they mean and how they are used, see the companion *Birds of Florida Audio CDs*.

BIRD BASICS

It's easier to identify birds and communicate about them if you know the names of the different parts of a bird. For instance, it's more effective to use the word "crest" to indicate the set of extra long feathers on top of a Northern Cardinal's head than to try to describe it.

The following illustration points out the basic parts of a bird. Because it is a composite of many birds, it shouldn't be confused with any actual bird.

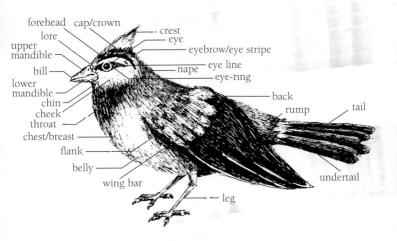

Bird Color Variables

No other animal has a color palette like a bird's. Brilliant blues, lemon yellows, showy reds and iridescent greens are commonplace within the bird world. In general, the male birds are more colorful than their female counterparts. This is probably to help the male attract a mate, essentially saying, "Hey, look at me!" It also calls attention to the male's overall health. The better the condition of his feathers, the better his food source and territory, and therefore the better his potential for a mate.

Female birds that don't look like their male counterparts (such species are called sexually dimorphic, meaning "two forms") are often a nondescript color, as seen with Boat-tailed Grackles. These muted tones help to hide the females during weeks of motionless incubation, and draw less attention to them when they are out feeding or taking a break from the rigors of raising their young.

In some species such as the Bald Eagle, Blue Jay and Downy Woodpecker, male birds look nearly identical to the females. In the case of woodpeckers, the sexes are differentiated by only a single red mark or sometimes a yellow mark. Depending upon the species, the mark may be on top of the head, face, nape of neck or just behind the bill.

During the first year, juvenile birds often look like the mothers. Since brightly colored feathers are used mainly for attracting a mate, young non-breeding males don't have a need for colorful plumage. It is not until the first spring molt (or several years later, depending on the species) that young males obtain their breeding colors.

Both breeding and winter plumages are the result of molting. Molting is the process of dropping old worn feathers and replacing them with new ones. All birds molt, typically twice a year, with the spring molt usually occurring in late winter. During this time, most birds produce their breeding plumage (brighter colors for attracting mates), which lasts throughout the summer.

Winter plumage is the result of the late summer molt, which serves a couple of important functions. First, it adds feathers for warmth in the coming winter season. Second, in some species it produces feathers that tend to be drab in color, which helps to camouflage the birds and hide them from predators. The winter plumage of the male American Goldfinch, for example, is olive brown unlike its obvious canary yellow color during summer. Luckily for us, some birds such as the male Northern Cardinal retain their bright summer colors all year long.

Bird Nests

Bird nests are truly an amazing feat of engineering. Imagine building your home strong enough to weather a storm, large enough to hold your entire family, insulated enough to shelter them from cold and heat, and waterproof enough to keep out rain. Now, build it without any blueprints or directions, and without the use of your hands or feet! Birds do!

Before building a nest, an appropriate site must be selected. In some species such as House Wrens, the male picks out several potential sites and assembles several small twigs in each. This discourages other birds from using nearby nest cavities. These "extra" nests are occasionally called dummy nests. The female is then taken around and shown all the choices. She chooses her favorite and finishes constructing the nest. In some other species of birds—Baltimore Orioles, for example--it is the female who chooses the site and constructs the nest, with the male offering only an occasional suggestion. Each species has its own nest-building routine, which is strictly followed.

As you'll see in the following illustrations, birds build a wide variety of nest types.

ground nest

platform nest

cup nest

pendulous nest

Nesting material often consists of natural elements found in the immediate area. Most nests consist of plant fibers (such as bark peeled from grapevines), sticks, mud, dried grass, feathers, fur, or soft fuzzy tufts from thistle. Some birds, including Ruby-throated Hummingbirds, use spider webs to glue nest materials together. Nesting material is limited to what a bird can hold or carry. Because of this, a bird must make many trips afield to gather enough materials to complete its nest. Most nests take at least four days or more, and hundreds, if not thousands, of trips to build.

The simple **ground nest** is scraped out of the earth. A shallow depression that usually contains no nesting material, it is made by birds such as the Killdeer and Black Skimmer.

Another kind of nest, the **platform nest**, represents a more complex type of nest building. Constructed of small twigs and branches, the platform nest is a simple arrangement of sticks which forms a platform and features a small depression to nestle the eggs.

Some platform nests, such as those of the Common Loon, are constructed on the ground and are made with mud and grass. Platform nests can also be on cliffs, bridges, balconies or even in flowerpots. This kind of nest gives space to adventurous youngsters and functions as a landing platform for the parents. Many waterfowl build platform nests on the ground, usually near water or actually in water. These floating platform nests vary with the water level, thus preventing nests with eggs from being flooded. Platform nests, constructed by such birds as Mourning Doves and herons, are not anchored to the tree and may tumble from the branches during high winds and storms.

The **cup nest** is a modified platform nest, used by three-quarters of all songbirds. Constructed from the outside in, a supporting platform is constructed first. This platform is attached firmly to a tree, shrub, rock ledge or the ground. Next, the sides are constructed of grasses, small twigs, bark or leaves, which are woven together and often glued with mud for added strength. The inner cup, lined with feathers, animal fur, soft plant material or animal hair, is constructed last. The mother bird uses her chest to cast the final contours of the inner nest.

The **pendulous nest** is an unusual nest, looking more like a sock hanging from a branch than a nest. Inaccessible to most predators, these nests are attached to the ends of the smallest branches of a tree and often wave wildly in the breeze. Woven very tightly of plant fibers, they are strong, watertight and take up to a week to construct. More commonly used by tropical birds, this complicated type of nest has also been mastered by orioles and kinglets. A small opening on the top or side allows the parents access to the grass-lined interior. (It must be one heck of a ride to be inside one of these nests during a windy spring thunderstorm!)

One of the most clever of all nest types is known as the **no nest** or daycare nest. Parasitic birds such as Brown-headed Cowbirds build no nests at all! The egg-laden female expertly searches out other birds' nests and sneaks in to lay one of her own eggs while the host mother is not looking, thereby leaving the host mother to raise an adopted youngster. The mother cowbird wastes no energy building a nest only to have it raided by a predator. By using several nests of other birds, she spreads out her progeny so at least one of her offspring will live to maturity.

Another type of nest, the **cavity nest**, is used by many bird species, including woodpeckers and Eastern Bluebirds. The cavity nest is usually excavated in a tree branch or trunk and offers shelter from storms, sun, predators and cold. A relatively small entrance hole in a tree leads to an inner chamber up to 10 inches (25 cm) below. Usually constructed by woodpeckers, the cavity nest is typically used only once by its builder, but subsequently can be used for many years by birds such as Tree

Swallows, mergansers and bluebirds, which do not have the capability of excavating one for themselves. Kingfishers, on the other hand, excavate a tunnel up to 4 feet (1 m) long, which connects the entrance in a riverbank to the nest chamber. These cavity nests are often sparsely lined because they are already well insulated.

Some birds, including some swallows, take nest building one step further. They use a collection of small balls of mud to construct an adobe-style home. Constructed beneath the eaves of houses, under bridges or inside chimneys, some of these nests look like simple cup nests. Others are completely enclosed, with small tunnel-like openings that lead into a safe nesting chamber for the baby birds.

Who Builds the Nest?

In general, the female bird builds the nest. She gathers nesting materials and constructs a nest, with an occasional visit from her mate to check on progress. In some species, both parents contribute equally to the construction of a nest. A male bird might forage for precisely the right sticks, grass or mud, but it is often the female that forms or puts together the nest. She uses her body to form the egg chamber. Rarely does the male build a nest by himself.

Fledging

Fledging is the interval between hatching and flight or leaving the nest. Some birds leave the nest within hours of hatching (precocial), but it might be weeks before they are able to fly. This is common with waterfowl and shorebirds. Until they start to fly, they are called fledglings. Birds that are still in the nest are called nestlings. Other baby birds are born naked and blind, and remain in the nest for several weeks (altricial).

Why Birds Migrate

Why do birds migrate? The short answer is simple–food. Birds migrate to areas with high concentrations of food, as it is easier to breed where food is than where it is not. A typical migrating bird–the Purple Martin, for instance–will migrate from the tropics of South America to nest in forests of North America, taking advantage of billions of newly hatched insects to feed its young. This trip is called **complete migration**.

Some birds of prey return from their complete migration to northern regions that are overflowing with small rodents such as mice and voles that have continued to breed in winter.

Complete migrators have a set time and pattern of migration. Each year at nearly the same time, they take off and head for a specific wintering ground–often Florida. Complete migrators may travel great distances, sometimes as much as 15,000 miles (24,150 km) or more in one year. But complete migration does not necessarily imply flying from the cold and frozen northland to a South American destination. The Baltimore Oriole, for example, is a complete migrator that flies from southern states with mild winters, such as Tennessee and Mississippi, to spend the winter in Florida. This is still called complete migration.

There are many interesting aspects to complete migrators. In the spring, males usually migrate several weeks before the females, arriving early to scope out possibilities for nesting sites and food sources, and to begin to defend territories. The females arrive several weeks later. In the autumn, in many species, the females and their young leave early, often up to four weeks before the adult males.

All migrators are not the same type. There are **partial migrators** such as American Goldfinches that usually wait until the food supply dwindles before flying south. Unlike complete migrators, the partial migrators move only far enough south, or sometimes east and west, to find abundant food. In some years it might be only a few hundred miles, while in other years it might be nearly a thousand. This kind of migration, dependent on the weather and available food, is sometimes called seasonal movement.

Unlike the predictable ebbing and flowing behavior of complete migrators or partial migrators, **irruptive migrators** can move every third to fifth year or, in some cases, in consecutive years. These migrations are triggered when times are really tough and food is scarce. Purple Finches are a good example of irruptive migrators, because they leave their normal northern range in search of food or in response to overpopulation.

How Do Birds Migrate?

One of the many secrets of migration is fat. While we humans are fighting the battle of the bulge, birds intentionally gorge themselves to put on as much fat as possible while still being able to fly. Fat provides the greatest amount of energy per unit of weight, and in the same way that your car needs gas, birds are propelled by fat and stalled without it.

During long migratory flights, fat deposits are used up quickly, and birds need to stop to "refuel." This is when backyard bird feeding stations and undeveloped, natural spaces around our towns and cities are especially important. Some birds require up to 2-3 days of constant feeding to build their fat reserves before continuing their seasonal trip.

Some birds such as most eagles, hawks, ospreys, falcons and vultures migrate during the day. Larger birds can hold more body fat, go longer without eating and take longer to migrate. These birds glide along on rising columns of warm air, called thermals, which hold them aloft while they slowly make their way north or south. They generally rest during the night and hunt early in the morning before the sun has a chance to warm the land and create good soaring conditions. Birds migrating during the day use a combination of landforms, rivers, and the rising and setting sun to guide them in the right direction.

Most other birds migrate during the night. Studies show that some birds which migrate at night use the stars to navigate. Others use the setting sun, while still others such as doves use the earth's magnetic fields to guide them north or south. While flying at night might seem like a crazy idea, nocturnal migration is safer for several reasons. First, there are fewer nighttime predators for migrating birds. Second, traveling at night allows time during the day to find food in unfamiliar surroundings. Finally, nighttime wind patterns tend to be flat, or laminar. These flat winds don't have the turbulence associated with daytime winds and can actually help carry smaller birds by pushing them along.

HOW TO USE THIS GUIDE

To help you quickly and easily identify birds, this field guide is organized by color. Simply note the color of the bird and turn to that section. Refer to the first page for the color key. The Red-headed Woodpecker, for example, is black and white with a red head. Because this bird is mostly black and white, it will be found in the black and white section. Each color section is also arranged by size, generally with the smaller birds first. Sections may also incorporate the average size in a range, which, in some cases, reflects size differences between male and female birds. Flip through the pages in that color section to find the bird. If you already know the name of the bird, check the index for the page number. In some species, the male and female are remarkably different in color. In others, the color of breeding and winter plumages differs. These species will have an inset photograph with a page reference and in most cases are found in two color sections.

In the description section you will find a variety of information about the bird. On page 1 is a sample of information included in the book.

Range Maps

Range maps are included for each bird. Colored areas indicate where in Florida a particular bird is most likely to be found. The colors represent the presence of a species during a specific season, not the density or amount of birds in the area. Green is used for summer, blue for winter, red for year-round and yellow for areas where the bird is seen during migration. While every effort has been made to accurately depict these ranges, they are only general guidelines. Ranges actually change on an ongoing basis due to a variety of factors. Changes in the weather, species abundance, landscape and vital resources such as availability of food and water can affect local populations, migration and movements, causing birds to be found in areas that are atypical for the species.

Colored areas simply mean bird sightings for that species have been frequent in those areas and less frequent in others. Please use the maps as intended—as general guides only.

Using the Companion *Birds of Florida Audio CDs*

The CD icon at the bottom of each description page includes a track number for the bird on the *Birds of Florida Audio CDs*. Play the track number to hear the bird's songs and calls. Bird songs and calls on the CDs are organized in the same order as the birds in the book. For species in which the male and female are different colors (sexually dimorphic) or when the breeding and winter plumage color differs, the birds are shown in the book in two color sections. On the CDs the recording of a species is presented only once and coincides with the first time the bird is shown in the book.

Common Name

YEAR-ROUND
MIGRATION
SUMMER
WINTER

Size: measures head to tail, may include wingspan

Male: a brief description of the male bird, and may include breeding, winter or other plumages

Female: a brief description of the female bird, which is sometimes not the same as the male

Juvenile: a brief description of the juvenile bird, which often looks like the female

Nest: the kind of nest this bird builds to raise its young; who builds the nest; how many broods per year

Eggs: how many eggs you might expect to see in a nest; color and marking

Incubation: the average time parents spend incubating the eggs; who does the incubation

Fledging: the average time young spend in the nest after hatching but before they leave the nest; who does the most "childcare" and feeding

Migration: complete (consistent, seasonal), partial (seasonal movement, destination varies), irruptive (unpredictable, depends on the food supply), non-migrator; additional comments

Food: what the bird eats most of the time (e.g., seeds, insects, fruit, nectar, small mammals, fish); if it typically comes to a bird feeding station

Compare: notes about other birds that look similar, and the pages on which they can be found

Stan's Notes: Interesting gee-whiz natural history information. This could be something to look or listen for, or something to help positively identify the bird. Also includes remarkable features.

female
pg. 121

male

Eastern Towhee
Pipilo erythrophthalmus

YEAR-ROUND

Size: 7-8" (18-20 cm)

Male: A mostly black bird with dirty red brown sides and white belly. Long black tail with white tip. Short, stout, pointed bill. White wing patches flash in flight. Off-white eyes.

Female: similar to male, but is brown, not black

Juvenile: light brown, a heavily streaked head, chest and belly, long dark tail with white tip

Nest: cup; female builds; 2 broods per year

Eggs: 3-4; creamy white with brown markings

Incubation: 12-13 days; female incubates

Fledging: 10-12 days; male and female feed young

Migration: non-migrator in Florida

Food: insects, seeds, fruit; visits ground feeders

Compare: Slightly smaller than the American Robin (pg. 239) and has a white belly. The Gray Catbird (pg. 233) lacks a black head and rusty sides. The Common Grackle (pg. 11) lacks a white belly and has a long thin bill.

Stan's Notes: Common name comes from its distinctive "tow-hee" call given by both sexes. Mostly known for its characteristic call that sounds like, "Drink-your-tea!" Seen hopping backward with both feet (bilateral scratching), raking up leaf litter for insects and seeds. The female broods, but male does the most feeding of young. In southern coastal states, some have red eyes; others have white eyes. White-eyed variety is found in Florida.

 CD 1, TRACK 2

female pg. 125

male

Brown-headed Cowbird
Molothrus ater

Size: 7½" (19 cm)

Male: A glossy black bird, reminiscent of the Red-winged Blackbird. Chocolate brown head with a pointed, sharp gray bill.

Female: dull brown bird with bill similar to male

Juvenile: similar to female, only dull gray color and a streaked chest

Nest: no nest; lays eggs in nests of other birds

Eggs: 5-7; white with brown markings

Incubation: 10-13 days; host bird incubates eggs

Fledging: 10-11 days; host birds feed young

Migration: non-migrator in Florida

Food: insects, seeds; will come to seed feeders

Compare: The male Red-winged Blackbird (pg. 9) is slightly larger with red and yellow patches on upper wings. Common Grackle (pg. 11) has a long tail and lacks the brown head. European Starling (pg. 7) has a shorter tail.

Stan's Notes: A member of the blackbird family. Of approximately 750 species of parasitic birds worldwide, this is the only parasitic bird in Florida, laying eggs in host birds' nests, leaving others to raise its young. Cowbirds are known to have laid eggs in nests of over 200 species of birds. Some birds reject cowbird eggs, but most incubate them and raise the young, even to the exclusion of their own. Look for warblers and other birds feeding young birds twice their own size. At one time cowbirds followed bison to feed upon insects attracted to the animals.

YEAR-ROUND

winter

breeding

YEAR-ROUND

European Starling
Sturnus vulgaris

Size: 7½" (19 cm)

Male: Gray-to-black bird with white speckles in fall and winter. Shiny purple black during spring and summer. Long, pointed yellow bill in spring turns gray in fall. Short tail.

Female: same as male

Juvenile: similar to adult, gray brown in color with a streaked chest

Nest: cavity; male and female line cavity; 2 broods per year

Eggs: 4-6; bluish with brown markings

Incubation: 12-14 days; female and male incubate

Fledging: 18-20 days; female and male feed young

Migration: non-migrator

Food: insects, seeds, fruit; comes to seed and suet feeders

Compare: Similar to Common Grackle (pg. 11), but lacks its long tail. The male Brown-headed Cowbird (pg. 5) has a longer tail.

Stan's Notes: A great songster, this bird can mimic other birds and sounds. Often displaces woodpeckers, chickadees and other cavity-nesting birds. Can be very aggressive and destroy eggs or young of other birds. Bill changes color with the seasons: yellow in spring, gray in autumn. Jaws are designed to be the most powerful when opening, as they pry open crevices to locate hidden insects. Gathers in the hundreds in autumn. Not a native bird, it was introduced to New York City in 1890-91 from Europe.

Thoosands,
Pinellas County

CD 1, TRACK 4

7

female pg. 135

male

YEAR-ROUND

Red-winged Blackbird
Agelaius phoeniceus

Size: 8½" (22 cm)

Male: Jet black bird with red and yellow shoulder patches on upper wings. Pointed black bill.

Female: heavily streaked brown bird with a pointed brown bill and white eyebrows

Juvenile: same as female

Nest: cup; female builds; 2-3 broods per year

Eggs: 3-4; bluish green with brown markings

Incubation: 10-12 days; female incubates

Fledging: 11-14 days, female and male feed young

Migration: partial to non-migrator in Florida

Food: seeds, insects; will come to seed feeders

Compare: Slightly larger than the male Brown-headed Cowbird (pg. 5), but is less iridescent and lacks the Cowbird's brown head. Differs from all other blackbirds due to the red and yellow patches on its wings (epaulets).

Stan's Notes: One of the most widespread and numerous birds in Florida. In autumn and winter, migrant and resident Red-wingeds gather in huge numbers (thousands) with other blackbirds to feed in agricultural fields, marshes and wetlands. Male defends territory by singing from tops of surrounding vegetation. Male repeats call from tops of cattails while showing off its red and yellow wing bars (epaulets). Female chooses a mate and often will nest over shallow water in thick stands of cattails. Red-wingeds feed mostly on seeds in fall and spring, switching to insects during summer.

Common Grackle
Quiscalus quiscula

YEAR-ROUND

Size: 11-13" (28-33 cm)

Male: Large black bird with iridescent blue black head, purple brown body, long black tail, long thin bill and bright golden eyes.

Female: similar to male, only duller and smaller

Juvenile: similar to female

Nest: cup; female builds; 2 broods per year

Eggs: 4-5; greenish white with brown markings

Incubation: 13-14 days; female incubates

Fledging: 16-20 days; female and male feed young

Migration: non-migrator to partial in Florida; moves around to find food

Food: fruit, seeds, insects; comes to seed feeders

Compare: Male Boat-tailed Grackle (pg. 17) is larger than the Common Grackle and has a much longer tail. The European Starling (pg. 7) is much smaller with a speckled appearance, and a yellow bill during breeding season. The male Red-winged Blackbird (pg. 9) has red and yellow wing markings (epaulets).

Stan's Notes: Usually nests in small colonies of up to 75 pairs, but travels with other blackbirds in large flocks. Is known to feed in farmers' fields. The name is derived from the Latin word *graculus*, meaning "to cough," for its loud raspy call. Male holds tail in a vertical keel-like position during flight. Flight pattern is almost always level, as opposed to an undulating up-and-down movement. Unlike most birds, it has larger muscles for opening the mouth (rather than for closing it) and prying crevices apart to locate hidden insects.

 CD 1, TRACK 6   common most places   11

YEAR-ROUND

Common Moorhen
Gallinula chloropus

Size: 14" (36 cm)

Male: Nearly black overall with yellow-tipped red bill. Red forehead. Thin line of white along sides. Yellowish green legs.

Female: same as male

Juvenile: same as adult, but brown with white throat and dirty yellow legs

Nest: ground; female and male build; 1-2 broods per year

Eggs: 2-10; brown with dark markings

Incubation: 19-22 days; female and male incubate

Fledging: 40-50 days; female and male feed young

Migration: non-migrator in Florida

Food: insects, snails, seeds

Compare: Similar size as the American Coot (pg. 15), which lacks the distinctive yellow-tipped bill and red forehead of Moorhen. Similar size as the Purple Gallinule (pg. 91), which has an iridescent blue and green body.

Stan's Notes: Also known as Mud Hen or Pond Chicken. A nearly all-black duck-like bird often seen in freshwater marshes and lakes. Walks on floating vegetation or swims while hunting for insects. Females known to lay eggs in other moorhen nests in addition to their own. Sometimes takes old nest in a low shrub. A cooperative breeder, having young of first brood help raise young of second. Young leave nest usually within a few hours after hatching, but stay with the family for a couple months. Young ride on backs of adults.

Coopers Bayou on
Bayshore Blvd

American Coot
Fulica americana

YEAR-ROUND
WINTER

Size: 13-16" (33-40 cm)

Male: Slate gray to black all over. White bill with a dark band near tip. Green legs and feet. A small white patch near the base of the tail. Prominent red eyes. Small red patch above bill between eyes.

Female: same as male

Juvenile: much paler than adult, with a gray bill and same white rump patch

Nest: cup; female and male build; 1 brood per year

Eggs: 9-12; pinkish buff with brown markings

Incubation: 21-25 days; female and male incubate

Fledging: 49-52 days; female and male feed young

Migration: non-migrator to complete in Florida

Food: insects, aquatic plants

Compare: Smaller than most other waterfowl. This is the only black water bird or duck-like bird with a white bill.

Stan's Notes: An excellent diver and swimmer, often seen in large flocks on open water. Not a duck, as it doesn't have webbed feet, but instead has large lobed toes. When taking off, scrambles across surface of water with wings flapping. Bobs head while swimming. Floating nests are anchored to vegetation. Huge flocks of as many as 1,000 birds gather for migration. The unusual common name "Coot" is of unknown origin, but in Middle English, *coote* was used to describe various waterfowl–perhaps it stuck. Like the Common Moorhen, the American Coot is also called Mud Hen.

female pg. 163

male

YEAR-ROUND

Boat-tailed Grackle
Quiscalus major

Size: 16" (40 cm), male
14" (36 cm), female

Male: Iridescent blue-black bird with a very long keel-shaped tail. Bright yellow eyes.

Female: brown version of male, lacks iridescence

Juvenile: similar to female

Nest: cup; female builds; 2 broods per year

Eggs: 2-4; pale greenish blue with brown marks

Incubation: 13-15 days; female incubates

Fledging: 12-15 days; female feeds young

Migration: non-migrator; moves around to find food

Food: insects, berries, seeds, fish; visits feeders

Compare: Similar to male Common Grackle (pg. 11), but male Boat-tailed has a distinctive long tail. Similar size as the Fish Crow (pg. 19) and the American Crow (pg. 21), but has a very different shape. Look for an iridescent blue head and a very long tail.

Stan's Notes: A noisy bird of coastal saltwater and inland marshes, giving several harsh, high-pitched calls and several squeaks. Eats a wide variety of foods from grains to fish. Sometimes seen picking insects off the backs of cattle. Will also visit bird feeders. Makes a cup nest with mud or cow dung and grass. Nests in small colonies. Most nesting occurs from February through July and occasionally again from October to December. Boat-taileds north of Gainesville have bright yellow eyes, but in the rest of the state the birds have dark eyes. More common in Florida than the Common Grackle, although less widespread.

Safety Harbor Pier

Fish Crow
Corvus ossifragus

YEAR-ROUND

Size: 16" (40 cm)

Male: All-black bird appearing nearly identical to the American Crow, but with a longer tail and smaller head and bill.

Female: same as male

Juvenile: same as adult

Nest: cup; female and male construct; 1 brood per year

Eggs: 4-5; blue or gray green with brown marks

Incubation: 16-18 days; female and male incubate

Fledging: 21-24 days; female and male feed young

Migration: non-migrator

Food: insects, carrion, mollusks, berries, seeds

Compare: Nearly identical to American Crow (pg. 21), but the Fish Crow is smaller, has a longer tail and a smaller head and bill. Fish Crow is most easily differentiated from American Crow by its higher-pitched call.

Stan's Notes: Essentially a bird of the coast and along major rivers, but can be found throughout Florida. Not uncommon for it to break open mollusk shells by dropping them onto rocks from above. Very sociable and gregarious. Nests in small colonies. Often builds a stick nest halfway up a tree. Forms small winter flocks of up to 100 birds, unlike American Crows, which usually form winter flocks of several hundred. The best way to distinguish between the two species is by their remarkably different calls. Fish Crow has a high, nasal "cah."

Thousands
Safety Harbor

in flight

American Crow
Corvus brachyrhynchos

YEAR-ROUND

Size: 18" (45 cm)

Male: All-black bird with black bill, legs and feet. Can have a purple sheen in direct sunlight.

Female: same as male

Juvenile: same as adult

Nest: platform; female builds; 1 brood per year

Eggs: 4-6; bluish to olive green with brown marks

Incubation: 18 days; female incubates

Fledging: 28-35 days; female and male feed young

Migration: non-migrator to partial

Food: fruit, insects, mammals, fish, carrion; will come to seed and suet feeders

Compare: Nearly identical to the Fish Crow (pg. 19), but American Crow is larger, has a shorter tail and a larger head and bill. American Crow is most easily differentiated from the Fish Crow by its lower-pitched call.

Stan's Notes: One of the most recognizable birds in Florida. Often reuses its nest every year if not taken over by a Great Horned Owl. Collects and stores bright, shiny objects in the nest. Able to mimic other birds and human voices. One of the smartest of all birds and very social, often entertaining itself by provoking chases with other birds. Feeds on road kill but is rarely hit by cars. Can live up to 20 years. Unmated birds known as helpers help raise the young. Large extended families roost together at night, dispersing during the day to hunt.

common

CD 1, TRACK 11

soaring

Black Vulture
Coragyps atratus

YEAR-ROUND

Size: 25" (63 cm); up to 4¾-foot wingspan

Male: Black vulture with dark gray head and legs. Short tail. In flight, all black with light gray wing tips.

Female: same as male

Juvenile: similar to adult

Nest: no nest on a stump or on ground, or takes an abandoned nest; 1 brood per year

Eggs: 2; light green with dark markings

Incubation: 37-48 days; female and male incubate

Fledging: 80-90 days; female and male feed young

Migration: non-migrator

Food: carrion, occasionally will capture small live mammals

Compare: Slightly smaller than the Turkey Vulture (pg. 25), lacking Turkey Vulture's bright red head. Turkey Vulture has two-toned wings, a black leading edge and light gray trailing edge. Black Vulture has shorter gray-tipped wings and shorter tail than Turkey Vulture.

Stan's Notes: Also called Black Buzzard. A more gregarious bird than the Turkey Vulture. In flight, the Black Vulture holds its wings straight out to its sides unlike the Turkey Vulture, which holds its wings in a V pattern. More aggressive while feeding but less skilled at finding carrion, it is thought Black Vulture's sense of smell is less developed than Turkey Vulture's. Families stay together for up to a year. Often nests and roosts with other Black Vultures. If startled, especially at the nest, it regurgitates with power and accuracy.

soaring

YEAR-ROUND

Turkey Vulture
Cathartes aura

Size: 26-32" (66-80 cm); up to 6-foot wingspan

Male: Large bird with obvious red head and legs. In flight, the wings appear two-toned: black leading edge with gray on the trailing edge and tip. The tips of wings end in finger-like projections. Long squared tail. Ivory bill.

Female: same as male

Juvenile: similar to adult, with gray-to-blackish head and bill

Nest: no nest, or minimal nest on cliff or in cave; 1 brood per year

Eggs: 2; white with brown markings

Incubation: 38-41 days; female and male incubate

Fledging: 66-88 days; female and male feed young

Migration: non-migrator in Florida

Food: carrion; parents regurgitate for young

Compare: Black Vulture (pg. 23) has shorter wings and tail. Bald Eagle (pg. 69) is larger and lacks two-toned wings. Unlike the Black Vulture and Bald Eagle, the Turkey Vulture holds its wings in a slight V during flight.

Stan's Notes: The vulture's naked head is an adaptation to reduce risk of feather fouling (picking up diseases) from carcasses. Unlike hawks and eagles, it has weak feet more suited to walking than grasping. One of the few birds that has a developed sense of smell. Mostly mute, making only grunts and groans. Seen in trees with wings outstretched, sunning itself. Recent studies show this bird is closely related to storks, not birds of prey.

 MUTE (not on CD)

Muscovy Duck
Cairina moschata

Size: 28" (71 cm)

Male: Wide range of color patterns from a glossy green-black to all white, with some being black and white (pied). Large bumpy patch of flesh, often red, around eyes and base of bill. Usually has a white wing patch, seen when perched and in flight.

Female: smaller than male, lacking the bumpy skin patch

Juvenile: same as adult, lacks the bumpy skin patch and white wing patch

Nest: ground; female builds; 1 brood per year

Eggs: 5-10; off-white without markings

Incubation: 25-27 days; female incubates

Fledging: 60-70 days; female shows the young what to eat

Migration: non-migrator

Food: aquatic insects, grass, seeds

Compare: Highly variable-colored duck that is easily identified by the bumpy skin patch around the eyes and base of bill.

Stan's Notes: A year-round Florida resident. Naturally occurring in Central and South America, it is a non-native duck that has been released in urban parks, ponds and lakes. Nests at base of trees and roosts in trees at night, like Wood Ducks. Not uncommon to nest near human dwellings under shrubbery. Can be very aggressive.

Naples Jan 2 Beach
Jan - Clearwater Executive GdfC

in flight

juvenile

drying

YEAR-ROUND
MIGRATION

Double-crested Cormorant
Phalacrocorax auritus

Size: 33" (84 cm)

Male: Large black water bird with a long snake-like neck. Long gray bill with yellow at the base and a hooked tip.

Female: same as male

Juvenile: lighter brown with a grayish chest and neck

Nest: platform, in colony; male and female build; 1 brood per year

Eggs: 3-4; bluish white without markings

Incubation: 25-29 days; female and male incubate

Fledging: 37-42 days; male and female feed young

Migration: non-migrator to complete in Florida

Food: small fish, aquatic insects

Compare: Male Anhinga (pg. 31) has white spots and streaks and a long straight bill without a hooked tip. The Turkey Vulture (pg. 25) is similar in size and also perches on branches with wings open to dry in sun, but it has a naked red head. American Coot (pg. 15) lacks the long neck and long pointed bill.

Stan's Notes: Often seen flying in large V formation. Usually roosts in large groups in trees close to water. Catches fish by swimming underwater with wings held at its sides. Lacks the oil gland that keeps feathers from becoming waterlogged. To dry off it strikes an erect pose with wings outstretched, facing the sun. Common name refers to its nearly invisible crests. "Cormorant" comes from the Latin *corvus*, meaning "crow," and *L. marinus*, meaning "pertaining to the sea," literally, "Sea Crow." *Ding Darling Reserve*

male

female

juvenile

Anhinga
Anhinga anhinga

Size: 35" (88 cm); up to 3¾-foot wingspan

Male: All black with glossy green and white spots and streaks on shoulders and wings. Long neck and tail. Long, narrow yellow bill.

Female: similar to male, buff brown neck and breast

Juvenile: similar to female, light brown-to-white body

Nest: platform; female and male build; 1 brood per year

Eggs: 2-4; light blue without markings

Incubation: 26-29 days; female and male incubate

Fledging: 21-25 days; female and male feed young

Migration: non-migrator in Florida

Food: fish, aquatic insects, crustaceans and small mammals

Compare: The Double-crested Cormorant (pg. 29) is slightly smaller and lacks the white spots and streaks of male Anhinga. Cormorant has a shorter bill with a curved tip unlike the long straight bill of the Anhinga.

Stan's Notes: Also called Snakebird due to its habit of appearing like a snake–surfacing with just its head and long thin neck showing above the water. It skewers fish, a favorite prey, with its long sharp bill. Unlike ducks and other diving birds, its feathers become waterlogged, which helps diving and maneuvering underwater. Afterward, it often strikes a pose with wings spread to dry in the sun. A strong flier frequently seen soaring, it is confused with birds of prey. In flight, the long neck and tail help to identify.

Dec   on Top of the World,
                              pond

male

female

Black-and-white Warbler
Mniotilta varia

Size: 5" (13 cm)

Male: Striped like a zebra, this small warbler has a distinctive black-and-white striped cap. White belly. Black chin and cheek patch.

Female: same as male, only duller and without the black chin and cheek patch

Juvenile: similar to female

Nest: cup; female builds; 1 brood per year

Eggs: 4-5; white with brown markings

Incubation: 10-11 days; female incubates

Fledging: 9-12 days; female and male feed young

Migration: complete, to Florida, Mexico, Central and South America

Food: insects

Compare: Look for the Black-and-white Warbler to creep down tree trunks headfirst, like the Brown-headed Nuthatch (pg. 207).

Stan's Notes: One of the first warblers to arrive in autumn and the only warbler that moves headfirst down a tree trunk. Look for it searching for insect eggs in the bark of large trees. Its song sounds like a slowly turning, squeaky wheel. Female performs a distraction dance to draw predators away from the nest. Constructs its nest on the ground, concealing it beneath dead leaves or at the base of a tree. Fall migrants arrive in August and depart in May. Found in a variety of habitats during winter. Doesn't nest in Florida.

CD 1, TRACK 15

male

female

YEAR-ROUND

Downy Woodpecker
Picoides pubescens

Size: 6" (15 cm)

Male: A small woodpecker with an all-white belly, black-and-white spotted wings, a black line running through the eyes, a short black bill, a white stripe down the back and red mark on the back of the head. Several small black spots along the sides of white tail.

Female: same as male, but lacks a red mark on head

Juvenile: same as female, some have a red mark near the forehead

Nest: cavity; male and female excavate; 1 brood per year

Eggs: 3-5; white without markings

Incubation: 11-12 days; female and male incubate, the female incubates during day, male at night

Fledging: 20-25 days; male and female feed young

Migration: non-migrator

Food: insects, seeds; visits seed and suet feeders

Compare: Almost identical to the Hairy Woodpecker (pg. 39), but smaller. Look for the shorter, thinner bill of Downy to differentiate them.

Stan's Notes: Abundant and widespread where trees are present. Stiff tail feathers help brace it like a tripod as it clings to a tree. Like all woodpeckers, it has a long barbed tongue to pull insects from tiny places. Male and female will drum on branches or hollow logs to announce territories, which are rarely larger than 5 acres (2 ha). Male performs most brooding. Will winter roost in cavity.

Honeymoon Island

male

female

Yellow-bellied Sapsucker

Sphyrapicus varius

WINTER

Size: 8-9" (20-22.5 cm)

Male: Medium-sized woodpecker with checkered back. Has a red forehead, crown and chin. Tan-to-yellow breast and belly. White wing patches flash while flying.

Female: similar to male, white chin

Juvenile: similar to female, dull brown and lacks any red marking

Nest: cavity; female and male excavate; 1 brood per year

Eggs: 5-6; white without markings

Incubation: 12-13 days; female and male incubate, the female incubates during day, male at night

Fledging: 25-29 days; female and male feed young

Migration: complete, to Florida, Mexico and Central America

Food: insects, tree sap; comes to suet feeders

Compare: The male Yellow-bellied Sapsucker shares the red chin of Red-headed Woodpecker (pg. 41), but lacks an all-red head. Female Yellow-bellied Sapsucker has a white chin.

Stan's Notes: Drills holes in a pattern of horizontal rows in small-to medium-sized trees to bleed tree sap. Many birds drink from sapsucker taps. Oozing sap also attracts insects, which sapsuckers eat. Sapsuckers will defend their sapping sites from the other birds. They don't suck sap; rather, they lap it with their long tongues. A quiet bird with few vocalizations, but will mew like a cat. Unlike other woodpeckers, drumming rhythm is irregular.

 CD 1, TRACK 17

male

female

YEAR-ROUND

Hairy Woodpecker
Picoides villosus

Size: 9" (22.5 cm)

Male: Black-and-white woodpecker with a white belly, and black wings with rows of white spots. White stripe down back. Long black bill. Red mark on back of head.

Female: same as male, but lacks a red mark on head

Juvenile: grayer version of female

Nest: cavity; female and male excavate; 1 brood per year

Eggs: 3-6; white without markings

Incubation: 11-15 days; female and male incubate, the female incubates during day, male at night

Fledging: 28-30 days; male and female feed young

Migration: non-migrator

Food: insects, nuts, seeds; comes to seed and suet feeders

Compare: Larger than Downy Woodpecker (pg. 35) and has a longer bill that is nearly the width of the head.

Stan's Notes: A common woodpecker of wooded backyards that announces its arrival with a sharp chirp before landing on feeders. This bird is responsible for eating many destructive forest insects. Has a barbed tongue, which helps it extract insects from trees. Tiny bristle-like feathers at the base of bill protect the nostrils from wood dust. Drums on hollow logs, branches or stovepipes in springtime to announce its territory. Often prefers to excavate nest cavities in live aspen trees. Has a larger, more oval-shaped cavity entrance than that of Downy Woodpecker.

 CD 1, TRACK 18

YEAR-ROUND

Red-headed Woodpecker
Melanerpes erythrocephalus

Size: 9" (22.5 cm)

Male: All-red head and a solid black back. White rump, chest and belly. Large white patches on wings flash when in flight. A black tail. Gray legs and bill.

Female: same as male

Juvenile: gray brown with white chest, lacks any red

Nest: cavity; male builds with help from female; 1 brood per year

Eggs: 4-5; white without markings

Incubation: 12-13 days; female and male incubate

Fledging: 27-30 days; female and male feed young

Migration: partial migrator; will move to areas with an abundant supply of nuts

Food: insects, nuts, fruit; comes to seed and suet feeders

Compare: No other woodpecker in Florida has an all-red head. The Pileated (pg. 61) is the only other woodpecker with a solid black back, but it has a partial red head.

Stan's Notes: One of the few woodpecker species in which male and female appear the same (look alike). Bill is not as well adapted for excavating holes as in other woodpeckers, so it chooses dead or rotten tree branches for nest. Later nesting than the closely related Red-bellied Woodpecker and will often take over its nesting cavity. Prefers more open or edge woodlands with many dead trees. Often seen perching on tops of dead snags. Stores acorns and other nuts. Nationwide populations are on the decrease.

male

female

Red-bellied Woodpecker
Melanerpes carolinus

YEAR-ROUND

Size: 9¼" (23 cm)

Male: "Zebra-backed" woodpecker with a white rump. Red crown extends down the nape of neck. Tan breast with a tinge of red on belly, which is often hard to see.

Female: same as male, but with a gray crown

Juvenile: gray version of adults, no red cap or nape

Nest: cavity; female and male excavate; 1 brood per year

Eggs: 4-5; white without markings

Incubation: 12-14 days; female and male incubate, the female incubates during day, male at night

Fledging: 24-27 days; female and male feed young

Migration: non-migrator; moves around to find food

Food: insects, nuts, fruit; comes to seed and suet feeders

Compare: Similar to Northern Flicker (pg. 153) and Yellow-bellied Sapsucker (pg. 37). Note the tan chest and belly with obvious black-and-white stripes on the back. The Red-headed Woodpecker (pg. 41) has an all-red head.

Stan's Notes: Named for its easily overlooked rosy red belly patch. Mostly a bird of shady woodlands. Excavates holes in rotten wood, looking for spiders, centipedes and beetles. Will hammer acorns and berries into crevices of trees for winter food. Returns to the same tree to excavate a new nest below that of the previous year. Often kicked out of nest hole by European Starlings. Gives a loud "querrr" call and a low "chug-chug-chug."

 CD 1, TRACK 20 Common in Florida

winter

breeding

Ruddy Turnstone
Arenaria interpres

MIGRATION
WINTER

Size: 9½" (24 cm)

Male: Breeding has orange legs, a black and white head marking, black bib, white breast and belly, black and chestnut wings and back. Slightly upturned black bill. Winter has a brown and white head and breast pattern.

Female: similar to male, only duller

Juvenile: similar to adults, but black and white head has a scaly appearance

Nest: ground; female builds; 1 brood per year

Eggs: 3-4; olive green with dark markings

Incubation: 22-24 days; male and female incubate

Fledging: 19-21 days; male feeds young

Migration: complete, to coastal Florida, South America

Food: aquatic insects, fish, mollusks, crustaceans, worms, eggs

Compare: Unusually ornamented shorebird. Look for a striking black and white pattern on head and neck, and orange legs to identify.

Stan's Notes: A common migrant and winter resident. Also called Rock Plover. Was named "Turnstone" because it turns stones over on rocky beaches to find food. Known for its unusual behavior of robbing and eating other birds' eggs. Will hang around crabbing operations to eat scraps from nets. Can be very tolerant of humans when feeding. Females often leave before their young leave the nests (fledge), resulting in males raising the young. Males have a bare spot on the belly (brood patch) to warm the young, something only females normally have.

Nov 22 2006   Daytona Beach Shores

winter pg. 247

breeding

Black-bellied Plover
Pluvialis squatarola

MIGRATION
WINTER

Size: 11-12" (28-30 cm)

Male: Striking black and white breeding plumage. A black belly, breast, sides, face and neck. White cap, nape of neck and belly near tail. Black legs and bill.

Female: less black on belly and breast than male

Juvenile: grayer than adults, with much less black

Nest: ground; male and female construct; 1 brood per year

Eggs: 3-4; pinkish or greenish with black brown markings

Incubation: 26-27 days; male and female incubate, male incubates during the day, female at night

Fledging: 35-45 days; male feeds young, young learn quickly to feed themselves

Migration: complete, to coastal Florida

Food: insects

Compare: The breeding Dunlin (pg. 131) is slightly smaller, with a rusty back and long down-curved bill. Look for a large black patch on the belly, face and chest and a white cap.

Stan's Notes: Males perform a "butterfly" courtship flight to attract females. Female leaves male and young about 12 days after the eggs hatch. Breeds at age 3. A winter resident along the Florida coast. Begins arriving in July and August (fall migration). During flight, in any plumage, displays a white rump and stripe on wings with black axillaries (armpits). Often darts across the ground to grab an insect and run.

 CD 1, TRACK 22

YEAR-ROUND
MIGRATION

Black-necked Stilt
Himantopus mexicanus

Size: 14" (36 cm)

Male: Upper parts of the head, neck and back are black. Lower parts are white. Ridiculously long red-to-pink legs. Long black bill.

Female: similar to male, only browner on back

Juvenile: similar to female, brown instead of black

Nest: ground; female and male construct; 1 brood per year

Eggs: 3-5; off-white with dark markings

Incubation: 22-26 days; female and male incubate, male incubates during the day, female at night

Fledging: 28-32 days; female and male feed young

Migration: complete to non-migrator in Florida

Food: aquatic insects

Compare: Outrageous length of the red-to-pink legs make this shorebird hard to confuse with any other.

Stan's Notes: Although a year-round resident in southern Florida, it can be found along the East coast and as far north as the Great Lakes. Usually leaves northern Florida during winter, but a few remain. Nests solitarily or in small colonies in open areas. This very vocal bird of shallow marshes gives a "kek-kek-kek" call. Its legs are up to 10 inches (25 cm) long and may be the longest legs in the bird world in proportion to the body. Known to transport water with water-soaked belly feathers (belly-soaking) to cool eggs in hot weather. Aggressively defends its nest, eggs and young. Young leave the nest shortly after hatching.

female pg. 169

male

Lesser Scaup
Aythya affinis

WINTER

Size: 16-17" (40-43 cm)

Male: Appears mostly black with bold white sides and gray back. Chest and head look nearly black, but head appears purple with green highlights in direct sun. Bright yellow eyes.

Female: overall brown with dull white patch at base of light gray bill, yellow eyes

Juvenile: same as female

Nest: ground; female builds; 1 brood per year

Eggs: 8-14; olive buff without markings

Incubation: 22-28 days; female incubates

Fledging: 45-50 days; female teaches young to feed

Migration: complete, to Florida, other southern states

Food: aquatic plants and insects

Compare: The male Ring-necked Duck (pg. 53) has a bold white ring on bill and lacks bold white sides. Male Blue-winged Teal (pg. 167) has a bright white crescent mark at base of bill.

Stan's Notes: Common diving duck in winter. Often in large flocks numbering in the thousands on lakes, ponds and sewage lagoons. Mostly seen during migration in October and late February. Prefers fresh water, but can be seen along the coast. Completely submerges itself to feed on the bottom of lakes (unlike dabbling ducks, which only tip forward to reach bottom). Note the bold white stripe under wings when in flight. Male leaves female when she starts incubating eggs. The quantity of eggs (clutch size) increases with the age of the female. Has an interesting baby-sitting arrangement in which groups of young (crèches) are tended by 1-3 adult females.

 CD 1, TRACK 24 Pond = Tierra Verde
SR 674

51

female pg. 173

male

WINTER

Ring-necked Duck
Aythya collaris

Size: 17" (43 cm)

Male: Striking duck with a black head, chest and back. Sides are gray to nearly white. A light blue bill with a bold white ring and second ring at base of bill. Top of head is peaked.

Female: dark brown back, light brown sides, a gray face, dark brown crown, white line behind eyes, white ring around a light blue bill, top of head is peaked

Juvenile: similar to female

Nest: ground; female builds; 1 brood per year

Eggs: 8-10; olive gray to brown without markings

Incubation: 26-27 days; female incubates

Fledging: 49-56 days; female teaches young to feed

Migration: complete, to Florida, other southern states

Food: aquatic plants and insects

Compare: Similar size as male Lesser Scaup (pg. 51), which has a gray back unlike the black back of the male Ring-necked Duck. Look for the prominent white ring around the bill of the male Ring-necked Duck.

Stan's Notes: One of the most abundant wintering ducks in the state. Usually seen in larger freshwater lakes rather than saltwater marshes. A diving duck, watch for it to dive underwater to forage for food. Takes to flight by springing up off water. Named "Ring-necked" because of the cinnamon collar (nearly impossible to see in the field). Also called Ring-billed Duck due to the white ring on its bill, and Blue Bill by duck hunters.

female pg. 175

male

Hooded Merganser
Lophodytes cucullatus

Size: 16-19" (40-48 cm)

Male: A sleek black-and-white bird that has rusty brown sides. Crest "hood" raises to reveal a large white patch. Long, thin black bill.

Female: sleek brown and rust bird with a ragged rusty crest and long, thin brown bill

Juvenile: similar to female

Nest: cavity; female lines old woodpecker hole; 1 brood per year

Eggs: 10-12; white without markings

Incubation: 32-33 days; female incubates

Fledging: 71 days; female feeds young

Migration: complete to non-migrator in Florida

Food: small fish, aquatic insects

Compare: A distinctive diving bird. Male Wood Duck (pg. 273) has a similar size and green head. Look for male Hooded Merganser's large white patch on head and rusty brown sides.

Stan's Notes: A small diving bird of shallow ponds, sloughs, lakes and rivers. Male Hooded Merganser can voluntarily raise and lower its crest to show off the large white head patch. Rarely found away from wooded areas, where it nests in natural cavities or nest boxes. Female will "dump" her eggs into other female Hooded Merganser nests, resulting in 20-25 eggs in some nests. Known to share nest cavities with Wood Ducks, sitting side by side.

On Top of World
pond

skimming

Black Skimmer
Rynchops niger

YEAR-ROUND
MIGRATION
WINTER

Size: 18" (45 cm); up to 3½-foot wingspan

Male: A striking black and white bird with black on top and white on bottom. Very distinct black-tipped red bill with lower bill longer than the upper. Red legs tuck up and out of sight when in flight.

Female: similar to male, only smaller

Juvenile: similar to adults, spotty brown on top

Nest: ground; female and male construct; 1 brood per year

Eggs: 3-5; bluish white with brown markings

Incubation: 21-23 days; female and male incubate

Fledging: 23-25 days; female and male feed young

Migration: non-migrator to complete in Florida

Food: small fish, shrimp

Compare: Royal Tern (pg. 307) has a similar shape, but lacks the black back and black-tipped red bill. No other large black and white bird skims across the water like Black Skimmer, and no other bird has a lower bill longer than the upper bill.

Stan's Notes: Also called Scissorbill or Razorbill, referring to this bird's unusual long bill. Uses its unique bill while in flight to cut through the water surface to catch fish or shrimp near the surface. Commonly feeds with several other skimmers. Often seen flying to and from nesting colony with fish in its bill. Nests in large colonies, often associated with terns. Found along the East and Gulf coasts.

Fort De Soto Park

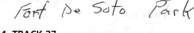

American Oystercatcher
Haematopus palliatus

Size: 18-19" (45-48 cm)

Male: Large shorebird with a large red-orange bill, black head and dark brown sides, wings and back. White chest and belly. Pink legs. Red ring around the eyes.

Female: same as male

Juvenile: more gray than black and lacks the brightly colored bill

Nest: ground; male and female construct; 1 brood per year

Eggs: 2-4; olive with sparse brown markings

Incubation: 24-29 days; male and female incubate, male incubates during the day, female at night

Fledging: 35-40 days; male and female feed young, young learn quickly to feed themselves

Migration: non-migrator to partial along coastal Florida

Food: shellfish, insects, aquatic insects, worms

Compare: Larger than breeding Black bellied Plover (pg. 47). Look for the large and obvious red-orange bill of Oystercatcher to identify.

Stan's Notes: This large, chunky shorebird has a flattened, heavy bill, which it uses to pry open shellfish and probe sand for insects and worms. Can be categorized according to its preferred oyster-opening technique. Stabbers sneak up on mollusks and stab their bills between shells before they have a chance to close. Hammerers shatter one-half of the shell with several direct, powerful blows.

male

female

YEAR-ROUND

Pileated Woodpecker
Dryocopus pileatus

Size: 19" (48 cm)

Male: Crow-sized woodpecker with a black back and bright red crest. Long gray bill with red mustache. White leading edge of the wings flashes brightly when flying.

Female: same as male, but has a black forehead and lacks red mustache

Juvenile: similar to adults, only duller and browner

Nest: cavity; male and female excavate; 1 brood per year

Eggs: 3-5; white without markings

Incubation: 15-18 days; female and male incubate, the female incubates during day, male at night

Fledging: 26-28 days; female and male feed young

Migration: non-migrator

Food: insects; will come to suet feeders

Compare: Red-headed Woodpecker (pg. 41) is about half the size and has an all-red head, black back and white rump. Look for the bright red crest and exceptionally large size of the Pileated Woodpecker.

Stan's Notes: Our largest woodpecker. The common name comes from the Latin *pileatus*, which means "wearing a cap," referring to its crest. A relatively shy bird that prefers large tracts of woodland. Drums on hollow branches, chimneys, etc., to announce territory. Excavates oval holes up to several feet long in tree trunks, looking for insects to eat. Large chips of wood lay at bases of excavated trees. Favorite food is carpenter ants. Young are fed regurgitated insects.

 CD 1, TRACK 29

in flight

SUMMER

Swallow-tailed Kite
Elanoides forficatus

Size: 23" (58 cm); up to 4-foot wingspan

Male: A white head, chest and belly. Black back, wings and tail. In flight, white leading edge of narrow pointed wings, a black trailing edge and a long, deeply forked tail. In the right light, black back and wings appear metallic green-blue.

Female: same as male

Juvenile: same as adult, but has a shorter tail

Nest: platform; female and male build; 1 brood per year

Eggs: 2-4; white with dark markings

Incubation: 26-28 days; female and male incubate

Fledging: 36-42 days; female and male feed young

Migration: complete, to Central and South America

Food: insects, snakes, lizards, frogs, mammals

Compare: Slightly smaller than the Osprey (pg. 65), which shares its black and white pattern. No other bird of prey in Florida has such a deeply forked tail.

Stan's Notes: Stunning in flight, the contrasting colors and forked tail easily identify it. Feeds while in flight. Also drinks on the wing, skimming across the surface of water like a swallow. Soars with its wings flat. Rarely hovers like other birds of prey. A very agile flyer, will collect sticks for nest like Ospreys by breaking off sticks with its feet as it flies. Semi-social, a couple of birds will share the same territory. Prefers open woods and river bottoms. Found mostly in Florida, range was once as far north as Minnesota.

soaring

Osprey
Pandion haliaetus

YEAR-ROUND

Size: 24" (60 cm); up to 5½-foot wingspan

Male: Large eagle-like bird with a white chest and belly and a nearly black back. White head with a black streak through the eyes. Large wings with black "wrist" marks. Dark bill.

Female: same as male, but larger with a necklace of brown streaking

Juvenile: similar to adults, with a light tan breast

Nest: platform, often on raised wooden platform; female and male build; 1 brood per year

Eggs: 2-4; white with brown markings

Incubation: 32-42 days; female and male incubate

Fledging: 48-58 days; male and female feed young

Migration: non-migrator to partial in Florida

Food: fish

Compare: Bald Eagle (pg. 69) is on average 10 inches (25 cm) larger with an all-white head and tail. The juvenile Bald Eagle is brown with white speckles. Look for a white belly and dark stripe through eyes to identify Osprey.

Stan's Notes: Ospreys are in a family all their own. It is the only raptor that plunges into water feet first to catch fish. Can hover for a few seconds before diving. Carries fish in a head-first position for better aerodynamics. Often harassed by Bald Eagles for its catch. In flight, wings are angled (cocked) backward. Nests on man-made towers and in tall dead trees. Recent studies show male and female might mate for life. May not migrate to same wintering grounds.

Common Honeymoon Island

20+ nesting p

Park

winter

breeding

Common Loon
Gavia immer

MIGRATION
WINTER

Size: 28-36" (71-90 cm)

Male: Breeding adult has a black-and-white back with a checkerboard pattern, a black head, white necklace, deep red eyes and a long, pointed black bill. Winter adult has an all-gray body and bill.

Female: same as male

Juvenile: similar to winter adult, lacks red eyes

Nest: platform, on the ground; female and male build; 1 brood per year

Eggs: 2; olive brown, occasionally brown markings

Incubation: 26-31 days; female and male incubate

Fledging: 75-80 days; female and male feed young

Migration: complete, to coastal Florida, other southern coastal states and Mexico

Food: fish, aquatic insects

Compare: Double-crested Cormorant (pg. 29) has a black chest and gray bill with yellow at the base and a hooked tip.

Stan's Notes: A true symbol of the wildness of our lakes. Prefers clear lakes because it hunts for fish by eyesight. Legs are set so far back that it has a difficult time walking on land, but it is a great swimmer. The common name comes from the Swedish word *lom*, meaning "lame," for the awkward way it walks on land. Its unique call suggests the wild laughter of a demented person and led to the phrase "crazy as a loon." Young ride on backs of swimming parents. Adults perform distraction displays to protect young. Very sensitive to disturbance during nesting and will abandon nest.

off Dunedin Causeway

soaring

juvenile

soaring
juvenile

Bald Eagle
Haliaeetus leucocephalus

YEAR-ROUND
MIGRATION

Size: 31-37" (79-94 cm); up to 7-foot wingspan

Male: Pure white head and tail contrast with dark brown-to-black body and wings. A large, curved yellow bill and yellow feet.

Female: same as male, only slightly larger

Juvenile: dark brown with white spots or speckles throughout body and wings, gray bill

Nest: massive platform, usually in a tree; female and male build; 1 brood per year

Eggs: 2; off-white without markings

Incubation: 34-36 days; female and male incubate

Fledging: 75-90 days; female and male feed young

Migration: non-migrator to partial, to the Southeast

Food: fish, carrion, birds (mainly ducks)

Compare: Larger than Black Vulture (pg. 23), which has a shorter tail and lacks the adult Bald Eagle's white head and tail. Turkey Vulture (pg. 25) is smaller and flies with its two-toned wings held in a V shape unlike the straight-out wing position of the Bald Eagle.

Stan's Notes: There are more Bald Eagles in Florida than in any other of the contiguous 48 states. Uses same nest year after year, adding more sticks, enlarging it to massive proportions, at times up to 1,000 pounds (450 kg). In the midair mating ritual, one eagle will flip upside down and lock talons with another. Both tumble, then break apart to continue flight. Thought to mate for life, but will switch mates if not successful reproducing. Juvenile attains the white head and tail at about 4-5 years of age. *Island*

3. Honeymoon hunting

Wood Stork
Mycteria americana

YEAR-ROUND
SUMMER

Size: 40" (102 cm); up to 5-foot wingspan

Male: An all-white body with a bald, nearly black head and thick, slightly down-curved dark bill. Tail, wing tips and entire trailing edge of wings are black, as seen in flight. Black legs and pink feet.

Female: same as male

Juvenile: similar to adult, but a gray-to-brown head and neck, dull yellow bill

Nest: platform; female and male build, 1 brood per year

Eggs: 2-4; white without markings

Incubation: 28-32 days; male and female incubate

Fledging: 55-60 days; female and male feed young

Migration: non-migrator to partial in Florida

Food: fish, amphibians, aquatic insects, snails

Compare: Similar size as Great Egret (pg. 317), which lacks Wood Stork's dark head and down-curved bill. Nearly twice the size of Snowy Egret (pg. 311). Look for a black tail, wing tips and trailing edge of wings during flight.

Stan's Notes: On state and federal endangered species lists. Like many wading birds, it has less than 20 percent of the population it had a century ago. Feeds by swinging its open bill through water until it contacts prey, then snaps bill shut. Shuffles its feet to stir up fish before capturing. Nests in large colonies, often high up in trees. Often doesn't breed until 4-5 years of age. Abandons eggs or young when food supply is short. *ON TOP OF The World*

YEAR-ROUND
WINTER

Blue-gray Gnatcatcher
Polioptila caerulea

Size: 4" (10 cm)

Male: A light blue-to-gray head, back, breast and wings, with a black forehead and eyebrows. White belly and prominent white eye-ring. Long black tail with a white undertail, often held cocked above the rest of body.

Female: same as male, only grayer and lacking black on the head

Juvenile: similar to female

Nest: cup; female and male construct; 1 brood per year

Eggs: 4-5; pale blue with dark markings

Incubation: 10-13 days; female and male incubate

Fledging: 10-12 days; female and male feed young

Migration: non-migrator to partial in Florida

Food: insects

Compare: The only small blue bird with a black tail. Very active near the nest, look for it flitting around upper branches in search of insects.

Stan's Notes: Seen throughout the state in a wide variety of forest types. Listen for its wheezy call notes to help locate. A fun and easy bird to watch. Flicks its tail up and down and from side to side while calling. Like many open woodland nesters, it is a common cowbird host. In many years, it nests so early that by mid-June it is no longer defending territory. Although the population is abundant and widespread, it has been decreasing in the recent past. Many northern Blue-gray Gnatcatchers winter in Florida.

YEAR-ROUND
MIGRATION

Tree Swallow
Tachycineta bicolor

Size: 5-6" (13-15 cm)

Male: Blue green during spring and greener in fall. Appears to change color in direct sunlight. White chin, breast and belly. Long, pointed wing tips. Notched tail.

Female: similar to male, only duller

Juvenile: gray brown with a white belly and grayish breast band

Nest: cavity; female and male line former woodpecker cavity or nest box; 1 brood per year

Eggs: 4-6; white without markings

Incubation: 13-16 days; female incubates

Fledging: 20-24 days; female and male feed young

Migration: non-migrator to partial in Florida

Food: insects

Compare: Similar color as Purple Martin (pg. 83), but smaller with a white breast and belly. The Barn Swallow (pg. 79) has a rust belly and deeply forked tail.

Stan's Notes: Most common at coastal beaches, freshwater ponds, lakes and agricultural fields. Can be attracted to your yard with a nest box. Competes with Eastern Bluebirds for cavities and nest boxes. Travels great distances to find dropped feathers to line its grass nest. Sometimes seen playing, chasing after dropped feathers. Often seen flying back and forth across fields, feeding upon insects. A year-round resident in Florida, gathering in large flocks during migration and winter.

Jan. 4 2007   Ding Darling Reserve Sanibel Island

female pg. 109

male

Indigo Bunting
Passerina cyanea

MIGRATION
SUMMER
WINTER

Size: 5½" (14 cm)

Male: Vibrant blue finch-like bird. Scattered dark markings on wings and tail.

Female: light brown bird with faint markings

Juvenile: similar to female

Nest: cup; female builds; 2 broods per year

Eggs: 3-4; pale blue without markings

Incubation: 12-13 days; female incubates

Fledging: 10-11 days; female feeds young

Migration: complete, to southern Florida, Mexico and Central and South America

Food: insects, seeds, fruit; will visit seed feeders

Compare: Male Eastern Bluebird (pg. 81) is larger and has a rusty red breast.

Stan's Notes: Usually only the males are noticed. Actually a black bird, as it doesn't have any blue pigment in its feathers. As with the Blue Jay, sunlight is refracted within the structure of the bunting's feathers, making them appear blue. Appears iridescent in direct sun. Molts to acquire body feathers with gray tips, which quickly wear off to reveal bright blue plumage in spring. Molts in fall to appear like females during winter. Males often sing from treetops to attract mates. Will come to feeders in spring before insects are plentiful. Mostly seen along woodland edges, feeding on insects. Migrates at night in flocks of 5-10 birds. Males return before the females and juveniles, usually returning to previous year's nest site. Juveniles move to within a mile from birth site.

MIGRATION
SUMMER

Barn Swallow
Hirundo rustica

Size: 7" (18 cm)

Male: A sleek swallow. Blue black back, cinnamon belly and reddish brown chin. White spots on a long, deeply forked tail.

Female: same as male, only slightly duller

Juvenile: similar to adults, with a tan belly and chin and a shorter tail

Nest: cup; female and male construct; 2 broods per year

Eggs: 4-5; white with brown markings

Incubation: 13-17 days; female incubates

Fledging: 18-23 days; female and male feed young

Migration: complete, to South America

Food: insects, prefers beetles, wasps and flies

Compare: Tree Swallow (pg. 75) has a white belly and chin and a notched tail. The Chimney Swift (pg. 97) has narrow pointed tail with wings longer than the body. The Purple Martin (pg. 83) is nearly 2 inches (5 cm) larger and has a dark purple belly.

Stan's Notes: Of the eight swallow species in Florida, this is the only one with a deeply forked tail. Unlike other swallows, the Barn Swallow rarely glides in flight, so look for continuous flapping. It builds a mud nest using up to 1,000 beak-loads of mud, often in or on barns. Nests in colonies of 4-6 individuals, but nesting alone isn't uncommon. Drinks in flight, skimming water or getting water from wet leaves. Also bathes while flying through rain or sprinklers.

Eastern Bluebird
Sialia sialis

YEAR-ROUND

Size: 7" (18 cm)

Male: Reminiscent of its larger cousin, American Robin, with a rusty red breast and a white belly. Sky blue head, back and tail.

Female: shares rusty red breast and white belly, but is grayer with faint blue tail and wings

Juvenile: similar to female, with spots on chest, blue wing markings

Nest: cavity, old woodpecker cavity or man-made nest box; female builds; 2 broods per year

Eggs: 4-5; pale blue without markings

Incubation: 12-14 days; female incubates

Fledging: 15-18 days; male and female feed young

Migration: non-migrator in most of Florida

Food: insects, fruit

Compare: Male Indigo Bunting (pg. 77) is nearly all blue, lacking the rusty red breast. Blue Jay (pg. 87) is much larger and has a crest.

Stan's Notes: Year-round resident that is joined by many northern migrants, swelling populations each winter. Once nearly eliminated from Florida due to a lack of nest cavities, bluebirds have made a remarkable comeback with the aid of bird enthusiasts who have put up thousands of bluebird nest boxes. Easily tamed. Will come to a shallow dish with mealworms. Bluebirds like open habitats such as fields, pastures and roadsides. Will perch in trees or on fence posts and wait for grasshoppers. Sings a distinctive "chur-lee chur chur-lee." Young of first brood help raise young of the second.

male

female

Purple Martin
Progne subis

Size: 8½" (22 cm)

Male: A large swallow-shaped bird with a purple head, back and belly. Black wings and tail. Notched tail.

Female: gray purple head and back with a whitish belly, darker wings and tail

Juvenile: same as female

Nest: cavity; female and male line cavity of house; 1 brood per year

Eggs: 4-5; white without markings

Incubation: 15-18 days; female incubates

Fledging: 26-30 days; male and female feed young

Migration: complete, to South America

Food: insects

Compare: The male is the only swallow with a dark purple belly. Usually seen only in groups.

Stan's Notes: The largest swallow species in North America. Once nested in tree cavities, but now nearly exclusively nests in man-made nest boxes throughout Florida. Main diet consists of dragonflies, not mosquitoes as once thought. Often drinks and bathes while flying by skimming water or flying through rain. Returns to the same nest site each year. Males arrive before the females and yearlings. Often nests within 100 feet (30 m) of a human dwelling and, in fact, the most successful colonies are located within this distance. Young strike out to form new colonies. Huge colonies gather in the fall to migrate to South America.

CD 1, TRACK 40

YEAR-ROUND

Florida Scrub-Jay
Aphelocoma coerulescens

Size: 11" (28 cm)

Male: A dark blue body with a lighter blue head. Dirty white belly, white forehead and a proportionately long tail.

Female: same as male

Juvenile: same as adult

Nest: cup; female and male construct; 1 brood per year

Eggs: 3-6; pale green with dark markings

Incubation: 15-17 days; female incubates

Fledging: 18-20 days; female and male feed young

Migration: non-migrator

Food: insects, fruit, seeds

Compare: The "other" jay in Florida. Darker blue than Blue Jay (pg. 87), and lacks Blue Jay's crest and black necklace. Look for the Scrub-Jay's white forehead and long tail to identify.

Stan's Notes: An indigenous species found in central Florida and nowhere else. Well known for its cooperative breeding system in which the young from one year help to raise the young of the new year. Has a wide variety of raspy, hoarse calls. Prefers a transitional scrubby habitat, usually of oak trees around 10 feet (3 m) tall with some openings. Not a backyard bird, like the Blue Jay. A threatened species, it has declined up to 90 percent in the twentieth century due to habitat loss.

CD 2, TRACK 41

Blue Jay
Cyanocitta cristata

Size: 12" (30 cm)

Male: Large, bright light blue and white bird with a black necklace. Crest moves up and down at will. White face with a gray belly. White wing bars on blue wings. Black spots and a white tip on blue tail.

Female: same as male

Juvenile: same as adult, only duller

Nest: cup; female and male construct; 1-2 broods per year

Eggs: 4-5; green to blue with brown markings

Incubation: 16-18 days; female incubates

Fledging: 17-21 days; female and male feed young

Migration: non-migrator to partial; moves around to find an abundant food source

Food: insects, fruit, carrion, seeds, nuts; comes to seed feeders, and ground feeders with corn

Compare: Slightly larger than the Florida Scrub-Jay (pg. 85), which is darker blue. The Eastern Bluebird (pg. 81) is much smaller and lacks the crest. Belted Kingfisher (pg. 89) lacks the vivid blue color and a black necklace.

Stan's Notes: Highly intelligent bird, solving problems, gathering food and communicating more than other birds. Will scream like a hawk to scatter birds at a feeder. Known as the alarm of the forest, screaming at intruders in woods. Known to eat eggs or young birds from the nests of other birds. One of the few birds to cache food. Feathers don't have blue pigment; refracted sunlight casts blue light.

common   Florida

YEAR-ROUND
WINTER

Belted Kingfisher
Ceryle alcyon

Size: 13" (33 cm)

Male: Large blue bird with white belly. Broad blue gray breast band and a ragged crest that is raised and lowered at will. Large head with a long, thick black bill. A small white spot directly in front of red brown eyes. Black wing tips with splashes of white that flash when flying.

Female: same as male, but with rusty breast band in addition to blue gray band, and rusty flanks

Juvenile: similar to female

Nest: cavity; female and male excavate; 1 brood per year

Eggs: 6-7; white without markings

Incubation: 23-24 days; female and male incubate

Fledging: 23-24 days; female and male feed young

Migration: complete to non-migrator in Florida

Food: small fish

Compare: Kingfisher is darker blue than the Blue Jay (pg. 87) and has a larger, more ragged crest. Kingfisher is rarely found away from water.

Stan's Notes: Seen perched on branches close to water, it will dive headfirst for small fish and return to a branch to eat. Has a loud machine-gun-like call. Excavates a deep cavity in bank of river or lake. Parents drop dead fish into water, teaching the young to dive. Regurgitates pellets of bone after meals, being unable to pass bones through the digestive tract. Mates recognize each other by call.

Common   Florida

Purple Gallinule
Porphyrio martinica

Size: 13" (33 cm)

Male: A vibrant blue head, breast and belly with iridescent green back and wings. Yellow-tipped red bill. White undertail. Yellow legs.

Female: same as male

Juvenile: brown version of adult, bronze legs

Nest: ground; female and male build; 1-2 broods per year

Eggs: 6-8; brown with dark markings

Incubation: 22-25 days; female and male incubate

Fledging: 55-60 days; female and male feed young

Migration: partial to non-migrator in Florida

Food: insects, snails, seeds, berries, frogs

Compare: Similar size as the American Coot (pg. 15), which lacks a yellow-tipped red bill. Similar in size to the Common Moorhen (pg. 13), but differentiated from it by the absence of a white side stripe. Look for a white undertail to help identify the Purple Gallinule.

Stan's Notes: This is one of Florida's most dramatic-looking birds, commonly seen in the Everglades. Uses its extremely long toes to walk on floating vegetation in freshwater and saltwater marshes, where it hunts for grasshoppers and other insects, grains and frogs. Family groups stay together, with the first brood sometimes helping to raise the second. Moves out of northern Florida during winter and can be seen year-round in the southern part of the state. Known for individuals to wander well north of Florida.

non-breeding adult

white juvenile

breeding

molting juvenile

Little Blue Heron
Egretta caerulea

[handwritten: ← Juvenile Ding Darling Sanibel]

Size: 24" (60 cm)

Male: Dark slate blue to purple nearly year-round. Breeding has several long plumes on crown with a reddish purple head and neck. Dull green legs, feet. Black-tipped blue-gray bill.

Female: same as male

Juvenile: pure white overall, yellowish legs and feet, black-tipped gray bill

Nest: platform; female and male build; 1 brood per year

Eggs: 2-6; light blue without markings

Incubation: 20-23 days; female and male incubate

Fledging: 42-49 days; female and male feed young

Migration: non-migrator to partial in Florida

Food: fish, aquatic insects

Compare: Breeding adult lacks the white belly of the Tricolored Heron (pg. 95). The juvenile is confused with the Snowy Egret (pg. 311), which has bright yellow feet, black legs and a solid black bill. The breeding Cattle Egret (pg. 309) has an orange buff crest, breast and back and a red-orange bill.

Stan's Notes: Unusual because young look completely different from adults. All-white young turn blotchy white the first year. By the second year they look like the adult birds. A very slow stalker of prey, feeding in freshwater lakes, rivers, saltwater marshes and wetlands. Nests in large colonies near saltwater sites. Often flies north after breeding season, returning to Florida for the winter.

YEAR-ROUND
SUMMER

[handwritten: Phillipe Park Safety Harbor]

Tricolored Heron
Egretta tricolor

Size: 26" (66 cm)

Male: Dark blue head, neck and wings contrast with a white belly and neck. Small brown patches at base of neck with lighter brown on the lower back. Long, slender yellow bill with a dark tip. Legs yellow to pale green.

Female: same as male

Juvenile: similar to adult, chestnut brown in place of dark blue areas

Nest: platform; female and male build; 1 brood per year

Eggs: 3-6; light blue without markings

Incubation: 21-25 days; female and male incubate

Fledging: 32-35 days; female and male feed young

Migration: non-migrator to partial in Florida

Food: fish, aquatic insects

Compare: Great Blue Heron (pg. 265) is much larger and lacks white undersides. The Little Blue Heron (pg. 93) is slightly smaller and lacks the yellow bill and white belly.

YEAR-ROUND
SUMMER

Stan's Notes: A medium-sized heron characterized by its white undersides. Like other herons, Tricolored has declined in numbers due to wetland habitat loss. To hunt, it stands still and waits. Will also chase after small fish. A year-round resident, although much less numerous in the winter. Seen mainly in saltwater marshes and estuaries, but also in freshwater marshes inland. Known to wander as far as Kansas. Colony nester with other herons, one adult always on duty at the nest. Was not hunted for plumes like other herons.

 CD 1, TRACK 46

Old Tampa Bay Phillipe Park

Chimney Swift
Chaetura pelagica

SUMMER

Size: 5" (13 cm)

Male: Nondescript, swallow-shaped bird, usually seen only in flight. Long, thin brown body with a pointed tail and head. Long swept-back wings are longer than body.

Female: same as male

Juvenile: same as adult

Nest: half cup; female and male build; 1 brood per year

Eggs: 4-5; white without markings

Incubation: 19-21 days; female and male incubate

Fledging: 28-30 days; female and male feed young

Migration: complete, to South America

Food: insects caught in air

Compare: Considerably smaller than Purple Martin (pg. 83) and lacks the iridescent purple of the Martin. The Barn Swallow (pg. 79) has a forked tail unlike the pointed tail of the Chimney Swift. Tree Swallow (pg. 75) has a white belly and blue green back.

Stan's Notes: One of the fastest fliers in the bird world. Spends all day flying, rarely perching. Bathes and drinks by skimming across water surfaces. Unique in-flight twittering call is often heard before bird is seen. Flies in groups, feeding on flying insects nearly 100 feet (30 m) in the air. Often called Flying Cigar due to its pointed body shape. Hundreds will nest and roost in large chimneys, hence the common name. Builds nest with tiny twigs, cementing it with saliva, attaching it to the inside of a chimney or hollow tree.

CD 1, TRACK 47

YEAR-ROUND
WINTER

Chipping Sparrow
Spizella passerina

Size: 5" (13 cm)

Male: Small gray brown sparrow with a clear gray breast, rusty crown and white eyebrows. A black eye line and thin gray black bill. Two faint wing bars.

Female: same as male

Juvenile: similar to adult, has a streaked breast, lacks the rusty crown

Nest: cup; female builds; 2 broods per year

Eggs: 3-5; blue green with brown markings

Incubation: 11-14 days; female incubates

Fledging: 10-12 days; female and male feed young

Migration: complete, to Florida, other southern states, Mexico and Central America

Food: insects, seeds; will come to ground feeders

Compare: Song Sparrow (pg. 105) is larger and has a heavily streaked breast. The female House Finch (pg. 101) has a streaked breast unlike the unmarked chest of Chipping Sparrow.

Stan's Notes: A winter resident in Florida, seen from October to May. A common garden or yard bird, often seen feeding on dropped seeds underneath feeders. Gathers in large family groups to feed in preparation for migration. Migrates at night in flocks of 20-30 birds. The common name comes from the male's slow "chip" call. Often is just called Chippy. Nest is placed low in dense shrubs and is almost always lined with animal hair. Can be very unafraid of people, allowing you to approach closely before it flies away.

male
pg. 289

female

House Finch
Carpodacus mexicanus

YEAR-ROUND

Size: 5" (13 cm)

Female: A plain brown bird with a heavily streaked white chest.

Male: orange red face, chest and rump, a brown cap, brown marking behind eyes, brown wings streaked with white, streaked belly

Juvenile: similar to female

Nest: cup, sometimes in cavities; female builds; 2 broods per year

Eggs: 4-5; pale blue, lightly marked

Incubation: 12-14 days; female incubates

Fledging: 15-19 days; female and male feed young

Migration: non-migrator to partial; will move around to find food

Food: seeds, fruit, leaf buds; will visit seed feeders

Compare: The female Purple Finch (pg. 111) is very similar, but has bold white eyebrows. The female American Goldfinch (pg. 323) has a clear chest and white wing bars.

Stan's Notes: Very social bird. Visits feeders in small flocks. Likes nesting in hanging flower baskets. Incubating female is fed by the male. Has a loud, cheerful warbling song. House Finches that were originally introduced to Long Island, New York, from the western U.S. in the 1940s have since populated the entire eastern U.S. Now found across the country. Can be the most common bird at feeders. Suffers from a fatal eye disease that causes the eyes to crust over.

 CD 1, TRACK 49

House Wren
Troglodytes aedon

WINTER

Size: 5" (13 cm)

Male: A small all-brown bird with lighter brown markings on tail and wings. Slightly curved brown bill. Often holds its tail erect.

Female: same as male

Juvenile: same as adult

Nest: cavity; female and male line just about any nest cavity; 2 broods per year

Eggs: 4-6; tan with brown markings

Incubation: 10-13 days; female and male incubate

Fledging: 12-15 days; female and male feed young

Migration: complete, to Florida, other southern states and Mexico

Food: insects, spiders, snails

Compare: House Wren is distinguished from Carolina Wren (pg. 107) by the lack of eyebrows. The long curved bill and long upturned tail differentiates House Wren from sparrows.

Stan's Notes: A prolific songster, it will sing from dawn until dusk during the mating season. Easily attracted to nest boxes. In spring, the male chooses several prospective nesting cavities and places a few small twigs in each. Female inspects each, chooses one, and finishes the nest building. She will completely fill the nest cavity with uniformly small twigs, then line a small depression at back of cavity with pine needles and grass. Often has trouble fitting long twigs through nest cavity hole. Tries many different directions and approaches until successful.

 CD 1, TRACK 50

Song Sparrow
Melospiza melodia

WINTER

Size:	5-6" (13-15 cm)
Male:	Common brown sparrow with heavy dark streaks on breast coalescing into a central dark spot.
Female:	same as male
Juvenile:	similar to adult, finely streaked breast, lacks a central spot
Nest:	cup; female builds; 2 broods per year
Eggs:	3-4; pale blue to green with reddish brown markings
Incubation:	12-14 days; female incubates
Fledging:	9-12 days; female and male feed young
Migration:	complete, to Florida, other southern states
Food:	insects, seeds; rarely visits seed feeders
Compare:	Similar to other brown sparrows. Look for a heavily streaked chest with central dark spot.

Stan's Notes: Many subspecies or varieties of Song Sparrow, but the dark central spot is found in each variant. Returns to a similar area each year, defending a small territory by singing from thick shrubs. This is a constant songster that repeats its loud, clear song every couple minutes. Song varies in structure, but is basically the same from region to region. A ground feeder, look for it to scratch at the same time with both feet ("double-scratch") to expose seeds. While the female builds another nest for a second brood, the male often takes over feeding the young. Unlike many other sparrow species, Song Sparrows rarely flock together. A common host of the Brown-headed Cowbird.

 CD 1, TRACK 51

Carolina Wren
Thryothorus ludovicianus

First (handwritten)

YEAR-ROUND

Size: 5½" (14 cm)

Male: Warm rusty brown head and back with an orange yellow chest and belly. White throat and a prominent white eye stripe. A short stubby tail, often cocked up.

Female: same as male

Juvenile: same as adult

Nest: cavity; female and male build; 2 broods per year, sometimes 3

Eggs: 4-6; white, sometimes pink or creamy, with brown markings

Incubation: 12-14 days; female incubates

Fledging: 12-14 days; female and male feed young

Migration: non-migrator

Food: insects, fruit, few seeds; visits suet feeders

Compare: Similar to House Wren (pg. 103), but the Carolina Wren is lighter brown and has a prominent white eye stripe.

Stan's Notes: Mates are long-term, remaining together throughout the year in permanent territories. Sings year-round. Male is known to sing up to 40 different song types, singing one song repeatedly before switching to another. Female also sings, resulting in duets. The male often takes over feeding the first brood while the female renests. Nests in birdhouses, unusual places such as in mailboxes, bumpers of cars or broken taillights, or in nearly any other cavity. Found in brushy yards or woodlands. *Early aim Song* (handwritten)

Jan 2007 (handwritten)

Safety Harbor (handwritten)

 CD 1, TRACK 52

female

male pg. 77

Indigo Bunting

Passerina cyanea

MIGRATION
SUMMER
WINTER

Size: 5½" (14 cm)

Female: Light brown finch-like bird. Faint streaking on a light tan chest. Wings have a very faint blue cast with indistinct wing bars.

Male: vibrant blue finch-like bird, scattered dark markings on wings and tail

Juvenile: similar to female

Nest: cup; female builds; 2 broods per year

Eggs: 3-4; pale blue without markings

Incubation: 12-13 days; female incubates

Fledging: 10-11 days; female feeds young

Migration: complete, to southern Florida, Mexico and Central and South America

Food: insects, seeds, fruit; will visit seed feeders

Compare: Female Indigo Bunting is similar to female finches. The female American Goldfinch (pg. 323) has white wing bars. The female Purple Finch (pg. 111) has white eyebrows and a heavily streaked breast. The female House Finch (pg. 101) also has a heavily streaked breast.

Stan's Notes: A secretive bird, usually only the male buntings are seen. Males often sing from treetops to attract mates. Will come to feeders in the spring before insects are plentiful. Mostly seen along woodland edges, feeding on insects. Migrates during the night in flocks of 5-10 birds. A late migrant, males return before the females and juveniles. Juveniles move to within a mile from birth site.

male pg. 291

female

Purple Finch
Carpodacus purpureus

WINTER

Size: 6" (15 cm)

Female: A plain brown bird with a heavily streaked chest. Prominent white eyebrows.

Male: raspberry red head, cap, breast, back and rump, brownish wings and tail

Juvenile: same as female

Nest: cup; female and male construct; 1 brood per year

Eggs: 4-5; greenish blue with brown markings

Incubation: 12-13 days; female incubates

Fledging: 13-14 days; female and male feed young

Migration: irruptive; moves around in winter in search of food

Food: seeds, insects, fruit; comes to seed feeders

Compare: Female House Finch (pg. 101) lacks female Purple Finch's white eyebrows. The female American Goldfinch (pg. 323) has a clear chest and white wing bars.

Stan's Notes: Usually seen only during winter in northern Florida, when flocks of Purple Finches leave their homes farther north and move around searching for food. Will visit seed feeders along with House Finches, making it difficult to tell them apart. Feeds mainly on seeds. Prefers open woods or woodland edges. Travels in flocks of up to 50. Has a rich loud song, with a distinctive "tic" note made only in flight. Not a purple color, the Latin species name *purpureus* means "crimson" or other reddish color.

 CD 1, TRACK 53

YEAR-ROUND

House Sparrow
Passer domesticus

Size: 6" (15 cm)

Male: Medium sparrow-like bird with large black spot on throat extending down to the chest. Brown back and single white wing bars. A gray belly and crown.

Female: slightly smaller than the male, light brown, lacks the throat patch and single wing bars

Juvenile: similar to female

Nest: domed cup nest, within cavity; female and male build; 2-3 broods per year

Eggs: 4-6; white with brown markings

Incubation: 10-12 days; female incubates

Fledging: 14-17 days; female and male feed young

Migration: non-migrator; moves around to find food

Food: seeds, insects, fruit; comes to seed feeders

Compare: Lacks the rusty crown of Chipping Sparrow (pg. 99). Look for male House Sparrow's black bib. Female has a clear breast and lacks a rusty crown.

Stan's Notes: One of the first bird songs heard in cities in spring. Familiar city bird, nearly always in small flocks. Introduced from Europe to Central Park, New York, in 1850. Now found throughout North America. These birds are not really sparrows, but members of the Weaver Finch family, characterized by their large, oversized domed nests. Constructs a nest containing scraps of plastic, paper and whatever else is available. An aggressive bird that will kill the young of other birds in order to take over a cavity.

winter pg. 215

breeding

Least Sandpiper
Calidris minutilla

MIGRATION
WINTER

Size: 6" (15 cm)

Male: Breeding plumage has a golden brown head and back. White eyebrows and belly. Dull yellow legs. Short, down-curved black bill.

Female: same as male

Juvenile: similar to winter adult, but buff brown and lacks the breast band

Nest: ground; male and female construct; 1 brood per year

Eggs: 3-4; olive with dark markings

Incubation: 19-23 days; male and female incubate

Fledging: 25-28 days; male and female feed young

Migration: complete, to coastal Florida, other southern coastal states, Mexico and Central America

Food: aquatic and terrestrial insects, seeds

Compare: The smallest of sandpipers. Often confused with breeding Western Sandpiper (pg. 117) and Semipalmated Sandpiper (pg. 217), Least Sandpiper's yellow legs differentiate it from other tiny sandpipers. The short, thin, down-curved bill also helps to identify.

Stan's Notes: A winter resident in coastal Florida. Also winters in other coastal states from the Carolinas to California. This is a tiny, tame sandpiper that can be approached without scaring. It is the smallest of peeps (sandpipers), nesting on the tundra in northern regions of Canada and Alaska. Prefers grassy flats of saltwater and freshwater ponds. Its yellow legs can be difficult to see in water, poor light or when covered with mud.

Jan 2009 Font De Soto Park

winter pg. 219

breeding

MIGRATION
WINTER

Western Sandpiper
Calidris mauri

Size: 6½" (16 cm)

Male: Breeding has a bright rust brown crown, ear patch and back and a white chin and chest. Black legs. Narrow bill that droops near tip.

Female: same as male

Juvenile: similar to breeding adult, bright buff brown on the back only

Nest: ground; male and female construct; 1 brood per year

Eggs: 2-4; light brown with dark markings

Incubation: 20-22 days; male and female incubate

Fledging: 19-21 days; male and female feed young

Migration: complete, to coastal Florida

Food: aquatic and terrestrial insects

Compare: Breeding Least Sandpiper (pg. 115) and Semipalmated Sandpiper (pg. 217) lack the bright rust brown cap, ear patch and back, and the Least lacks black legs. Western has a longer bill that droops slightly at the tip.

Stan's Notes: A winter resident in coastal Florida. Also winters in other coastal states from the Carolinas to California. Nests on the ground in large "loose" colonies on the tundra of northern coastal Alaska. Adults leave the breeding grounds several weeks before the young. Some obtain breeding plumage before leaving the state in spring. Feeds on insects at the water's edge, sometimes immersing its head. Will feed in deeper water than Semipalmated Sandpipers. Young leave the nest (precocial) within a few hours after hatching. Female leaves and the male tends the hatchlings.

Semipalmated Plover
Charadrius semipalmatus

MIGRATION
WINTER

Size: 7" (18 cm)

Male: A brown-backed bird with a black necklace and short, black-tipped orange bill. White patch on forehead. White breast and belly. Breeding plumage has a black mask and an orange eye-ring around each eye.

Female: same as male

Juvenile: similar to adult, lacks a well-defined black necklace

Nest: ground; male builds; 1 brood per year

Eggs: 3-4; light brown with dark markings

Incubation: 23-25 days; male and female incubate

Fledging: 22-28 days; male and female feed young

Migration: complete, to coastal Florida

Food: insects, seeds, worms

Compare: Smaller than the Killdeer (pg. 149), which shares the brown back and white belly but has 2 black neck bands. Look for a very short bill and single black necklace to help identify the Semipalmated Plover.

Stan's Notes: Winter resident along coastal Florida. Also winters in other coastal states from the Carolinas to California. Often in mixed flocks with Semipalmated Sandpipers. Hunts by running quickly, stopping to look, then stabbing prey. Breeding birds usually have orange eye-rings. Prefers to nest in open rocky places, where the male will scrape out a shallow depression. Nests on the ground on the tundra of Alaska and northern Canada. Population decreased dramatically during the late 1800s due to hunting.

male
pg. 3

female

Eastern Towhee
Pipilo erythrophthalmus

YEAR-ROUND

Size: 7-8" (18-20 cm)

Female: A mostly light brown bird. Rusty red brown sides and white belly. Long brown tail with white tip. Short, stout, pointed bill. White wing patches flash in flight. Off-white eyes.

Male: similar to female, but is black, not brown

Juvenile: light brown, a heavily streaked head, chest and belly, long dark tail with white tip

Nest: cup; female builds; 2 broods per year

Eggs: 3-4; creamy white with brown markings

Incubation: 12-13 days; female incubates

Fledging: 10-12 days; male and female feed young

Migration: non-migrator in Florida

Food: insects, seeds, fruit; visits ground feeders

Compare: Slightly smaller than the American Robin (pg. 239), which has a red chest unlike the white chest and belly of Eastern Towhee.

Stan's Notes: Common name comes from its distinctive "tow-hee" call given by both sexes. Mostly known for its characteristic call that sounds like, "Drink-your-tea!" Seen hopping backward with both feet (bilateral scratching), raking up leaf litter for insects and seeds. The female broods, but male does the most feeding of young. In southern coastal states, some have red eyes; others have white eyes. White-eyed variety is found in Florida.

1 year old

Bohemian
Waxwing

Cedar Waxwing
Bombycilla cedrorum

WINTER

Size: 7½" (19 cm)

Male: Very sleek-looking gray-to-brown bird with pointed crest, light yellow belly and bandit-like black mask. Tip of tail is bright yellow and the tips of wings look as if they have been dipped in red wax.

Female: same as male

Juvenile: grayish with a heavily streaked chest, lacks red wing tips, black mask and sleek look

Nest: cup; female and male construct; 1 brood per year, occasionally 2

Eggs: 4-6; pale blue with brown markings

Incubation: 10-12 days; female incubates

Fledging: 14-18 days; female and male feed young

Migration: partial migrator; moves around to find food

Food: cedar cones, fruit, insects

Compare: Similar to its larger, less common cousin, Bohemian Waxwing (see inset), which has white on wings and rust under tail. Female Cardinal (pg. 133) has a large red bill.

Stan's Notes: The name is derived from its red wax-like wing tips and preference for eating small blueberry-like cones of the cedar. Mostly seen in flocks, moving from area to area, looking for berries. Wanders in winter to find available food supplies. During summer, before berries are abundant, it feeds on insects. Spends most of its time at the tops of tall trees. Listen for the very high-pitched "sreee" whistling sounds it constantly makes. Obtains mask after first year and red wing tips after second year.

 CD 1, TRACK 58

male pg. 5

female

YEAR-ROUND

Brown-headed Cowbird
Molothrus ater

Size: 7½" (19 cm)

Female: Dull brown bird with no obvious markings. Pointed, sharp gray bill.

Male: glossy black bird, chocolate brown head

Juvenile: similar to female, only dull gray color and a streaked chest

Nest: no nest, lays eggs in nests of other birds

Eggs: 5-7; white with brown markings

Incubation: 10-13 days; host bird incubates eggs

Fledging: 10-11 days; host birds feed young

Migration: non-migrator in Florida

Food: insects, seeds; will come to seed feeders

Compare: Female Red-winged Blackbird (pg. 135) is slightly larger and has white eyebrows and a streaked chest. European Starling (pg. 7) has speckles and a shorter tail.

Stan's Notes: A member of the blackbird family. Of approximately 750 species of parasitic birds worldwide, this is the only parasitic bird in Florida, laying eggs in host birds' nests, leaving others to raise its young. Cowbirds are known to have laid eggs in nests of over 200 species of birds. Some birds reject cowbird eggs, but most incubate them and raise the young, even to the exclusion of their own. Look for warblers and other birds feeding young birds twice their own size. At one time cowbirds followed bison to feed upon insects attracted to the animals.

breeding

winter

MIGRATION
WINTER

Spotted Sandpiper

Actitis macularius

Flock of 10-12 (handwritten)

Size:	8" (20 cm)
Male:	Olive brown back. Long bill and long dull yellow legs. White line over eyes. Breeding plumage has black spots on a white chest and belly. Winter has a clear chest and belly.
Female:	same as male
Juvenile:	similar to winter adult, with a darker bill
Nest:	ground; female and male build; 2 broods per year
Eggs:	3-4; brownish with brown markings
Incubation:	20-24 days; male incubates
Fledging:	17-21 days; male feeds young
Migration:	complete, to coastal Florida
Food:	aquatic insects
Compare:	Smaller than Lesser Yellowlegs (pg. 143). Killdeer (pg. 149) has 2 black neck bands. Look for Spotted Sandpiper to bob its tail up and down while standing. Look for the breeding Spotted Sandpiper's black spots extending from chest to belly.

Stan's Notes: This is one of the more common sandpipers. One of the few shorebirds that will dive underwater when pursued. Can fly straight up out of the water. Flies with wings held in a cup-like arc, rarely lifting them above a horizontal plane. Constantly bobs its tail while standing and walks as if delicately balanced. Female mates with multiple males and lays eggs in up to five different nests. Male incubates and cares for young. In winter plumage, it lacks the black spots on chest and belly.

Dec 2000 (handwritten)
Campbell Courtney (handwritten)
Causeway (handwritten)

winter pg. 229

breeding

Sanderling
Calidris alba

MIGRATION
WINTER

Size: 8" (20 cm)

Male: Breeding season (April to August) plumage has a rusty head, chest and back with white belly. Black legs and bill.

Female: same as male

Juvenile: spotty black on the head and back, a white belly, black legs and bill

Nest: ground; male builds; 1-2 broods per year

Eggs: 3-4; greenish olive with brown markings

Incubation: 24-30 days; male and female incubate

Fledging: 16-17 days; female and male feed young

Migration: complete, to coastal Florida, other southern coastal states, Mexico and Central America

Food: insects

Compare: Spotted Sandpiper (pg. 127) is the same size as Sanderling, but the breeding Spotted Sandpiper has black spots on its chest.

Stan's Notes: One of the most common shorebirds in the state, but mostly seen in its gray winter plumage from August to April. Can be seen in groups on sandy beaches, running out with each retreating wave to feed. Look for a flash of white on wings when it's in flight. Sometimes a female mates with several males (polyandry), which results in males and the female incubating separate nests. Both sexes perform a distraction display when threatened. Nests on the Arctic tundra. Rests while standing on one leg (see inset) and tucking the other leg into its belly feathers. Often hops away on one leg, moving away from pedestrians on the beach. Surveys show a greater than 80 percent decline in numbers since the 1970s.

common Beaches Fla

winter
pg. 231

breeding

MIGRATION
WINTER

Dunlin
Calidris alpina

Size: 8-9" (20-22.5 cm)

Male: Breeding adult is distinctive with a rusty red back, finely streaked chest and an obvious black patch on the belly. Stout bill, curving slightly downward at the tip. Black legs.

Female: slightly larger than male, with a longer bill

Juvenile: slightly rusty back with a spotty chest

Nest: ground; male and female construct; 1 brood per year

Eggs: 2-4; olive buff or blue green with red brown markings

Incubation: 21-22 days; male and female incubate, male incubates during the day, female at night

Fledging: 19-21 days; male feeds young, female often leaves before young fledge

Migration: complete, to coastal Florida, other southern coastal states, Mexico and Central America

Food: insects

Compare: Similar in size to the breeding Sanderling (pg. 129), look for the obvious black belly patch and curved bill of breeding Dunlin.

Stan's Notes: Breeding plumage more commonly seen in spring. Flights include heights of up to 100 feet (30 m) with brief gliding alternating with shallow flutters, and a rhythmic, repeating song. Huge flocks fly synchronously, with birds twisting and turning, flashing light and dark undersides. Males tend to fly farther south in winter than females. Winter visitor along the coast. Doesn't nest in Florida.

Fort De Soto Park

Jan. 2007

female

male pg. 295

juvenile

YEAR-ROUND

Northern Cardinal
Cardinalis cardinalis

Size: 8-9" (20-22.5 cm)

Female: Buff brown bird with tinges of red on crest and wings, a black mask and large red bill.

Male: red bird with a black mask extending from face down to chin and throat, large red bill and crest

Juvenile: same as female, but with a blackish gray bill

Nest: cup; female builds; 2-3 broods per year

Eggs: 3-4; bluish white with brown markings

Incubation: 12-13 days; female and male incubate

Fledging: 9-10 days; female and male feed young

Migration: non-migrator

Food: seeds, insects, fruit; comes to seed feeders

Compare: The Cedar Waxwing (pg. 123) has a small dark bill. Female Cardinal appears similar to the juvenile Cardinal, but juvenile has a dark bill. Look for the bright red bill of the female Northern Cardinal.

Stan's Notes: A familiar backyard bird. Look for the male feeding female during courtship. Male feeds young of the first brood by himself while female builds second nest. The name comes from the Latin word *cardinalis*, which means "important." Very territorial in spring, it will fight its own reflection in a window. Non territorial during winter, gathering in small flocks of up to 20 birds. Both the female and male sing and can be heard anytime of year. Listen for its "whata-cheer-cheer-cheer" territorial call in spring.

male pg. 9

female

Red-winged Blackbird
Agelaius phoeniceus

YEAR-ROUND

Size:	8½" (22 cm)
Female:	Heavily streaked brown bird with a pointed brown bill and white eyebrows.
Male:	jet black bird with red and yellow patches on upper wings, pointed black bill
Juvenile:	same as female
Nest:	cup; female builds; 2-3 broods per year
Eggs:	3-4; bluish green with brown markings
Incubation:	10-12 days; female incubates
Fledging:	11-14 days; female and male feed young
Migration:	partial to non-migrator in Florida
Food:	seeds, insects; will come to seed feeders
Compare:	Female Brown-headed Cowbird (pg. 125) is smaller and lacks the white eyebrows and heavily streaked breast.

Stan's Notes: One of the most widespread and numerous birds in Florida. In autumn and winter, migrant and resident Red-wingeds gather in huge numbers (thousands) with other blackbirds to feed in agricultural fields, marshes and wetlands. Male defends territory by singing from tops of surrounding vegetation. Male repeats call from tops of cattails while showing off its red and yellow wing bars (epaulets). Female chooses a mate and often will nest over shallow water in thick stands of cattails. Red-wingeds feed mostly on seeds in fall and spring, switching to insects during summer.

SUMMER

Common Nighthawk
Chordeiles minor

Size: 9" (22.5 cm)

Male: A camouflaged brown and white bird with white chin. A distinctive white band across wings and the tail, seen only in flight.

Female: similar to male, but with tan chin, lacks the white tail band

Juvenile: similar to female

Nest: no nest; lays eggs on the ground, usually on rocks, or on rooftop; 1 brood per year

Eggs: 2; cream with lavender markings

Incubation: 19 20 days; female and male incubate

Fledging: 20-21 days; female and male feed young

Migration: complete, to South America

Food: insects caught in air

Compare: Much larger than Chimney Swift (pg. 97) and smaller than the Chuck-will's-widow (pg. 157), which lacks the white chin and wing band. Look for obvious white wing band of Nighthawk in flight, and characteristic flap-flap-flap-glide flight pattern.

Stan's Notes: Usually only seen flying at dusk or after sunset, but it is not uncommon for it to be seen sitting on a fence post, sleeping during the day. A very noisy bird, repeating a "peenting" call during flight. Alternates slow wing beats with bursts of quick wing beats. Prolific insect eater. Prefers gravel rooftops for nesting in cities and nests on the ground in the country. Male's distinctive springtime mating ritual is a steep diving flight terminated with a loud popping noise. One of the first birds to migrate each autumn.

YEAR-ROUND

Burrowing Owl
Athene cunicularia

Size: 9½" (24 cm); up to 21-inch wingspan

Male: A brown owl with bold white spots, white belly and very long legs. Yellow eyes.

Female: same as male

Juvenile: same as adult, but belly is brown

Nest: cavity, former underground mammal den; female and male line den; 1 brood per year

Eggs: 6-11; white without markings

Incubation: 21-28 days; female incubates

Fledging: 25-28 days; female and male feed young

Migration: non-migrator in southern Florida

Food: insects, mammals, lizards, birds

Compare: Eastern Screech-Owl (pg. 237) is slightly smaller and has ear tufts. Burrowing Owl is less than half the size of Great Horned Owl (pg. 191), which has feather tuft "horns." Burrowing spends most of its time on the ground unlike tree-loving Great Horned.

Stan's Notes: An owl of fields, open backyards, golf courses and airports. Nests in small family units or in small colonies. Takes over the underground dens of mammals, occasionally widening its den by kicking dirt backward. Lines den with cow pies, horse dung, grass and feathers. Some people have had success attracting these owls to their backyards by creating artificial dens. Often seen in the day, standing or sleeping around den entrance. Male brings food to incubating female, often moving family to a new den when young are just a few weeks old. Will bob head up and down while doing deep knee bends when agitated or threatened.

YEAR-ROUND

Northern Bobwhite
Colinus virginianus

Size: 10" (25 cm)

Male: Short, stocky, mostly brown bird with short gray tail. A prominent white eye stripe and white chin. Reddish brown sides and belly, often with black lines and dots.

Female: similar to male, with buff brown eye stripe and chin

Juvenile: smaller and duller than adults

Nest: ground; female and male construct; 1 brood per year

Eggs: 12-15; white to creamy without markings

Incubation: 23-24 days; female and male incubate

Fledging: 6-7 days; female and male feed young

Migration: non-migrator

Food: insects, seeds, fruit; will come to ground feeders offering corn and millet

Compare: Mourning Dove (pg. 155) is light brown and has a long pointed tail.

Stan's Notes: Most common in northern Florida. Prefers shrubs, orchards, hedgerows and pastures. Moves around in small flocks of 20 birds (often family members), called a covey. The covey often rests together at night, in a tight circle with tails together and heads facing outward, to watch for predators. Males and females perform distraction displays when nests or young are threatened. Nest is a depression in the ground lined with grass. Frequently pulls nearby vegetation over nest to help conceal it. Male gives a rising whistle, "bob-white," heard mainly in spring and summer. Will also give a single "hoy" call year-round.

Lesser Yellowlegs
Tringa flavipes

Jan 4 2007

MIGRATION
WINTER

Size: 10-11" (25-28 cm)

Male: A typical sandpiper-type bird with a brown back and wings and lightly streaked white breast and belly. Thin, straight black bill. Long yellow legs.

Female: same as male

Juvenile: same as adult

Nest: ground; female builds; 1 brood per year

Eggs: 3-4; yellowish with brown markings

Incubation: 22-23 days; male and female incubate

Fledging: 18-20 days; male and female lead young to food

Migration: complete, to Florida and South America

Food: aquatic insects, tiny fish

Compare: Greater Yellowlegs (pg. 161) has a longer, upturned bill. Breeding Willet (pg. 165) has brown legs. Breeding Spotted Sandpiper (pg. 127) has black spots on its chest.

Stan's Notes: Usually seen in small flocks, it combs shorelines and mud flats looking for aquatic insects. Most often seen in the head down, tail up position, walking along, looking to snatch up food. Uses its long straight bill to pluck insects and tiny fish from water. Very shy bird that quite often moves into the water prior to taking flight. Has a variety of "flight" notes that it gives when taking off. A member of the group of sandpipers called Tattlers, all of which scream alarm calls when taking flight. Nests on marshes in spruce forests of central Alaska and central Canada. The nest is a simple depression atop a mound of earth.

Sanibel Ding Darling Reserve

winter pg. 245

breeding

Short-billed Dowitcher
Limnodromus griseus

YEAR-ROUND
MIGRATION

Size: 11" (28 cm)

Male: Breeding plumage is an overall rusty brown with heavy black spots throughout. Has a small amount of white very low on belly. A long, straight black bill. Off-white eyebrow stripe. Dull yellow-to-green legs and feet.

Female: same as male

Juvenile: similar to winter adult

Nest: ground; female and male construct; 1 brood per year

Eggs: 3-4; olive green with dark markings

Incubation: 20-21 days; male and female incubate

Fledging: 25-27 days; male and female feed young

Migration: complete to non-migrator in Florida

Food: insects, snails, worms, leeches, seeds

Compare: Marbled Godwit (pg. 177) is larger and has a two-toned, upturned bill and gray legs. Smaller than the breeding Willet (pg. 165), which has a shorter bill, and bold black and white wing linings, as seen in flight.

Stan's Notes: A common year-round resident found along coastal Florida and inland on freshwater lakes and marshes. With a rapid probing action like a sewing machine, it uses its long straight bill to probe deep into sand and mud for insects. Can be seen with the less common Long-billed Dowitcher (not shown), but it is difficult to tell the two apart.

Jan 2007   Fort De Soto

Sanibel   Ding Darling Preserve

Brown Thrasher
Toxostoma rufum

YEAR-ROUND

Size: 11" (28 cm)

Male: A rusty red bird with long tail and heavily streaked breast and belly. Two white wing bars. Long curved bill. Bright yellow eyes.

Female: same as male

Juvenile: same as adult, but eye color is grayish

Nest: cup; female and male construct; 2 broods per year

Eggs: 4-5; pale blue with brown markings

Incubation: 11-14 days; female and male incubate

Fledging: 10-13 days; female and male feed young

Migration: non-migrator in Florida

Food: insects, fruit

Compare: Similar shape as American Robin (pg. 239) and Gray Catbird (pg. 233), but the Brown Thrasher is slightly larger and has a streaked breast, rusty color and yellow eyes.

Stan's Notes: A prodigious songster, often in thick shrubs where it sings deliberate musical phrases, repeating each twice. Male has the largest documented song repertoire of all North American birds, with over 1,100 song types. Often seen quickly flying or running in and out of dense shrubs. Noisy feeding due to habit of turning over leaves, small rocks and branches. Seen year-round in Florida. Populations increase during the winter months with the influx of northern birds.

Killdeer

Charadrius vociferus

Nov 24/2006 Flock 20-30

Safety Harbor OLD IAMPA BAY Pier

YEAR-ROUND

Size: 11" (28 cm)

Male: An upland shorebird that has 2 black bands around the neck like a necklace. A brown back and white belly. Bright reddish orange rump, visible in flight.

Female: same as male

Juvenile: similar to adult, with 1 neck band

Nest: ground; male builds; 2 broods per year

Eggs: 3-5; tan with brown markings

Incubation: 24-28 days; male and female incubate

Fledging: 25 days; male and female lead their young to food

Migration: non-migrator in Florida

Food: insects

Compare: The Spotted Sandpiper (pg. 127) is found around water and lacks the 2 neck bands of the Killdeer. Semipalmated Plover (pg. 119) shares the brown back and white belly, but is smaller and has a single black necklace.

Stan's Notes: The only shorebird with two black neck bands. It is known for its broken wing impression, which draws intruders away from nest. Once clear of the nest, the Killdeer takes flight. Nests are only a slight depression in a gravel area, often very difficult to see. Young look like yellow cotton balls on stilts when first hatched, but quickly molt to appear similar to parents. Able to follow parents and peck for insects soon after birth. Is technically classified as a shorebird, but doesn't live at the shore. Often found in vacant fields or along railroads. Has a very distinctive "kill-deer" call.

 CD 2, TRACK 7

American Kestrel
Falco sparverius

YEAR-ROUND
WINTER

Size: 10-12" (25-30 cm); up to 2-foot wingspan

Male: Rusty brown back and tail. A white breast with dark spots. Double black vertical lines on white face. Blue gray wings. Distinctive wide black band with a white edge on tip of rusty tail.

Female: similar to male, but slightly larger, has rusty brown wings and dark bands on tail

Juvenile: same as adult of the same sex

Nest: cavity; doesn't build a nest within; 1 brood per year

Eggs: 4-5; white with brown markings

Incubation: 29-31 days; male and female incubate

Fledging: 30-31 days; female and male feed young

Migration: complete to non-migrator in Florida

Food: insects, small mammals and birds, reptiles

Compare: Similar to other falcons. Look for 2 vertical black stripes on the Kestrel's face. No other small bird of prey has a rusty back and tail.

Stan's Notes: A falcon that was once called Sparrow Hawk due to its small size. Could be called Grasshopper Hawk because it eats many grasshoppers. Can see ultraviolet light; this ability helps it locate mice and other small mammals by their urine, which glows bright yellow in ultraviolet light. Hovers near roads before diving for prey. Adapts quickly to a wooden nest box. Has pointed swept-back wings, seen in flight. Perches nearly upright. Unusual raptor in that males and females have quite different markings. Watch for them to pump their tails up and down after landing on perches.

male

female

Northern Flicker
Colaptes auratus

YEAR-ROUND

Size: 12" (30 cm)

Male: Brown and black woodpecker with a large white rump patch visible only when flying. Black necklace above a speckled breast. Red spot on nape of neck. Black mustache.

Female: same as male, but lacks a black mustache

Juvenile: same as adult of the same sex

Nest: cavity; female and male excavate; 1 brood per year

Eggs: 5-8; white without markings

Incubation: 11-14 days; female and male incubate

Fledging: 25-28 days; female and male feed young

Migration: non-migrator in Florida

Food: insects, especially ants and beetles

Compare: The male Yellow-bellied Sapsucker (pg. 37) is smaller and has a red chin and forehead. The male Red-bellied Woodpecker (pg. 43) has a red crown, a black-and-white zebra-striped back and lacks a mustache. Flickers are the only brown-backed woodpeckers in the state.

Stan's Notes: This is the only woodpecker to regularly feed on the ground. Preferring ants and beetles, it produces an antacid saliva to neutralize the acidic defense of ants. Male usually selects nest site, taking up to 12 days to excavate. Some have had success attracting flickers to nest boxes stuffed with sawdust. In flight, flashes golden yellow under wings and tail, undulates deeply and calls "wacka-wacka" loudly. Populations swell in winter with northern migrants.

 CD 2, TRACK 9

Safety Harbor

Mourning Dove
Zenaida macroura

YEAR-ROUND

Size: 12" (30 cm)

Male: Smooth fawn-colored dove with gray patch on the head. Iridescent pink, green around neck. A single black spot behind and below eyes. Black spots on wings and tail. Pointed wedge-shaped tail with white edges.

Female: similar to male, lacking iridescent pink and green neck feathers

Juvenile: spotted and streaked

Nest: platform; female and male build; 2 broods per year

Eggs: 2; white without markings

Incubation: 13-14 days; male and female incubate, male incubates during the day, female at night

Fledging: 12-14 days; female and male feed young

Migration: non-migrator in Florida

Food: seeds; will visit seed and ground feeders

Compare: White-winged Dove (pg. 243) has a white edge on the wings. Eurasian Collared-Dove (pg. 251) has a black collar. Lacks the color combinations of the Rock Pigeon (pg. 253).

Stan's Notes: Name comes from its mournful cooing. A ground feeder, bobbing its head as it walks. One of the few birds to drink without lifting its head, same as Rock Pigeon. Parents feed young, called squab, a regurgitated liquid called crop-milk for the first few days of life. Flimsy platform nest of twigs often falls apart during a storm. Wind rushing through wing feathers during flight creates a characteristic whistling sound.

common in Florida

YEAR-ROUND
SUMMER

Chuck-will's-widow
Caprimulgus carolinensis

Size: 12" (30 cm)

Male: Mottled brown and black throughout with a thin light tan necklace. Tiny bill and long rounded tail. White tail feathers are hidden.

Female: same as male, lacks the white tail feathers

Juvenile: same as adult

Nest: no nest; 1 brood per year

Eggs: 1-2; off-white with dark markings

Incubation: 20-24 days; female incubates

Fledging: 17-20 days; female feeds young

Migration: complete to non-migrator in Florida

Food: insects caught in air

Compare: Rarely seen due to its nocturnal behavior. Common Nighthawk (pg. 137) is smaller, has a white stripe across each wing (seen in flight) and a throat patch.

Stan's Notes: Usually is only heard and rarely seen. Gives a loud, repetitive, incessant call at night each spring and summer, "chuck-will's-widow." Most common in mixed oak and pine forest, where it lays its eggs directly on the ground, often in the same place each year. Will dart out from the nesting area (flush) if disturbed. Often roosts by perching parallel along the length of a branch, unlike other birds which roost diagonally on a branch. A tiny bill, but an enormous wide mouth (gape) to capture insects while in flight. More common in Florida than the Common Nighthawk. Related to Whip-poor-will (not shown), which is more common in northern states. Year-round resident in southern Florida, but most migrate farther south to Central and South America.

 CD 2, TRACK 11

winter

breeding

YEAR-ROUND

Pied-billed Grebe
Podilymbus podiceps

Size: 13" (33 cm)

Male: Small brown water bird with a black chin and black ring around a thick, chicken-like ivory bill. Puffy white patch under the tail. Has an unmarked brown bill during winter.

Female: same as male

Juvenile: paler than adult, with white spots and gray chest, belly and bill

Nest: floating platform; female and male build; 1 brood per year

Eggs: 5-7; bluish white without markings

Incubation: 22-24 days; female and male incubate

Fledging: 22-24 days; female and male feed young

Migration: non-migrator in Florida

Food: crayfish, aquatic insects, fish

Compare: Look for a puffy white patch under the tail and thick, chicken-like bill to help identify.

Stan's Notes: A very common water bird, usually seen diving for food. Slowly sinks like a submarine when disturbed. Sinks without diving by quickly compressing feathers to force air out. Was called Hell-diver because of the length of time it can stay submerged. Can surface far from where it went under. Very sensitive to pollution. Well suited to life on water, with short wings, lobed toes, and legs set close to the rear of its body. While swimming is easy, it is very awkward on land. Builds nest on a floating mat in water. "Grebe" probably came from the Old English word *krib*, meaning "crest," a reference to the crested head plumes of many grebes, especially during breeding season. *Ding Darling Reserve*

Common Sanibel

WINTER

Greater Yellowlegs
Tringa melanoleuca

Size: 14" (36 cm)

Male: Tall bird with a bulbous head and long thin bill, slightly upturned. Gray streaking on chest. White belly. Long yellow legs.

Female: same as male

Juvenile: same as adult

Nest: ground; female builds; 1 brood per year

Eggs: 3-4; off-white with brown markings

Incubation: 22-23 days; female and male incubate

Fledging: 18 20 days; male and female feed young

Migration: complete, to Florida, other southern states

Food: small fish, aquatic insects

Compare: Nearly identical to the Lesser Yellowlegs (pg. 143), only larger and has an upturned, longer bill. Has a longer neck and smaller head than breeding Willet (pg. 165), lacks Willet's distinctive black and white wing linings and has bright yellow legs.

Stan's Notes: A common shorebird that can be identified by the slightly upturned bill and long yellow legs. Often seen resting on one leg. Its long legs carry it through deep water. Feeds by rushing forward through the water, plowing its bill or swinging it from side to side, catching small fish and insects. A skittish bird quick to give an alarm call, causing flocks to take flight. Quite often moves into the water prior to taking flight. Has a variety of "flight" notes that it gives when taking off. Nests on the ground close to water on the northern tundra of Labrador and Newfoundland. Migrates earlier than Lesser Yellowlegs in spring and later in fall.

 CD 2, TRACK 13

female

male pg. 17

YEAR-ROUND

Boat-tailed Grackle
Quiscalus major

Size: 14" (36 cm), female
16" (40 cm), male

Female: A golden brown chest and head with nearly black wings and tail, lacking iridescence.

Male: iridescent blue-black bird with a very long tail and bright yellow eyes

Juvenile: similar to female

Nest: cup; female builds; 2 broods per year

Eggs: 2-4; pale greenish blue with brown marks

Incubation: 13-15 days; female incubates

Fledging: 12-15 days; female feeds young

Migration: non-migrator; moves around to find food

Food: insects, berries, seeds, fish; visits feeders

Compare: Fairly distinctive. Not confused with many other birds. Found only along the coast.

Stan's Notes: A noisy bird of coastal saltwater and inland marshes, giving several harsh, high-pitched calls and several squeaks. Eats a wide variety of foods from grains to fish. Sometimes seen picking insects off the backs of cattle. Will also visit bird feeders. Makes a cup nest with mud or cow dung and grass. Nests in small colonies. Most nesting occurs from February through July and occasionally again from October to December. Boat-taileds north of Gainesville have bright yellow eyes, but in the rest of the state the birds have dark eyes. More common in Florida than the Common Grackle, although less widespread.

Safety Harbor Pier

 CD 1, TRACK 9

breeding

winter pg. 255

displaying

YEAR-ROUND
WINTER

Willet
Catoptrophorus semipalmatus

Size: 15" (38 cm)

Male: Brown breeding plumage with a brown bill and legs. White belly. Distinctive black and white wing lining pattern, seen in flight or during display.

Female: same as male

Juvenile: similar to breeding adult, more tan in color

Nest: ground; female builds; 1 brood per year

Eggs: 3-5; olive green with dark markings

Incubation: 24-28 days; male and female incubate

Fledging: unknown days; female and male feed young

Migration: non-migrator to complete in coastal Florida

Food: aquatic insects

Compare: The Lesser Yellowlegs (pg. 143) and Greater Yellowlegs (pg. 161) have yellow legs. The Killdeer (pg. 149) has 2 black bands on the neck. Marbled Godwit (pg. 177) has a two-toned, upturned bill. Breeding Short billed Dowitcher (pg. 145) has yellow green legs.

Stan's Notes: Common along coastal Florida during winter, with many continuing to migrate through the state to the coast of South America. Appears a rich, warm brown during breeding season and rather plain gray during winter, but always has a striking black and white wing pattern when seen in flight. Uses its black and white wing patches to display to its mate. Named for the "pill-will-willet" call it gives during the breeding season. Gives a "kip-kip-kip" alarm call when it takes flight. Nests on the East and Gulf coasts, in some western states and Canada. Beaches – Dunedin Causeway

 CD 2, TRACK 14

male

female

Blue-winged Teal

Anas discors

WINTER

Jan 4 | 2007
Flock 30-40

Size: 15-16" (38-40 cm)

Male: Small, plain-looking brown duck speckled with black. A gray head with a large white crescent-shaped mark at base of bill. Black tail with small white patch. Blue wing patch (speculum), usually seen only in flight.

Female: duller version of male, lacks facial crescent mark and white patch on tail, showing only slight white at base of bill

Juvenile: same as female

Nest: ground; female builds; 1 brood per year

Eggs: 8-11; creamy white

Incubation: 23-27 days; female incubates

Fledging: 35-44 days; female feeds young

Migration: complete, to Florida, other southern states

Food: aquatic plants, seeds, aquatic insects

Compare: Male Blue-winged has a distinct white face marking. Female Wood Duck (pg. 181) and Mallard (pg. 199) are larger than the female Teal, and the Wood Duck has a crest.

Stan's Notes: One of the smallest ducks in North America and one of the longest distance migrating ducks, with widespread nesting as far north as Alaska. One of the most widespread and abundant winter ducks in Florida. Arrives in August, leaves in April and May. Constructs nest some distance from the water. Female performs a distraction display to protect her nest and young. Male leaves the female near the end of incubation. Planting crops and cultivating to pond edges have caused a decline in population.

Ding Darling Reserve
Sanibel Bay

male pg. 51

female

WINTER

Lesser Scaup
Aythya affinis

Size: 16-17" (40-43 cm)

Female: Overall brown duck with dull white patch at base of light gray bill. Yellow eyes.

Male: white and gray, the chest and head appear nearly black but head appears purple with green highlights in direct sun, yellow eyes

Juvenile: same as female

Nest: ground; female builds; 1 brood per year

Eggs: 8-14; olive buff without markings

Incubation: 22-28 days; female incubates

Fledging: 45-50 days; female teaches young to feed

Migration: complete, to Florida, other southern states

Food: aquatic plants and insects

Compare: Female Ring-necked Duck (pg. 173) has a white ring on bill. Male Blue-winged Teal (pg. 167) has a crescent-shaped white mark at the base of bill. The female Wood Duck (pg. 181) is larger with white around eyes.

Stan's Notes: Common diving duck in winter. Often in large flocks numbering in the thousands on lakes, ponds and sewage lagoons. Mostly seen during migration in October and late February. Prefers fresh water, but can be seen along the coast. Completely submerges itself to feed on the bottom of lakes (unlike dabbling ducks, which only tip forward to reach bottom). Note the bold white stripe under wings when in flight. Male leaves female when she starts incubating eggs. The quantity of eggs (clutch size) increases with the age of the female. Has an interesting baby-sitting arrangement in which groups of young (crèches) are tended by 1-3 adult females.

 CD 1, TRACK 24   Pond – Tierra Verde   169

soaring

YEAR-ROUND

Red-shouldered Hawk
Buteo lineatus

Size: 15-19" (38-48 cm); up to 3½-ft. wingspan

Male: Reddish (cinnamon) head, shoulders, chest and belly. Wings and back are dark brown with white spots. Long tail with thin white bands and wide black bands. Obvious red wing linings, seen in flight.

Female: same as male

Juvenile: similar to adult, lacks the cinnamon color, has a white chest with dark spots

Nest: platform; female and male build; 1 brood per year

Eggs: 2-4; white with dark markings

Incubation: 27-29 days; female and male incubate

Fledging: 39-45 days; female and male feed young

Migration: non-migrator to partial

Food: reptiles, amphibians, large insects, birds

Compare: Red-tailed Hawk (pg. 187) is much larger and has a white chest. Sharp-shinned Hawk (pg. 249) is smaller and lacks the reddish head and belly of Red-shouldered Hawk.

Stan's Notes: Common woodland hawk in Florida, seen in backyards. Prefers to hunt along edges of forest, spotting snakes, frogs, insects, an occasional small bird and other prey as it perches. Often seen flapping with an alternating gliding pattern. Very vocal hawk with a distinct scream. Mates when 2-3 years old. Stays in the same territory for many years. Starts building its nest in February. Young leave the nest by June.

Kapok Park - Clearwater
Jan 26/2007

male pg. 53

female

WINTER

Ring-necked Duck
Aythya collaris

Size: 17" (43 cm)

Female: Mainly brown back with light brown sides, a gray face and dark brown crown. White eye-ring extends into a line behind eye. A white ring around a light blue bill. Top of head is peaked.

Male: black head, breast and back, sides are gray to nearly white, a bold white ring around a light blue bill and second ring at the base of bill, top of head is peaked

Juvenile: similar to female

Nest: ground; female builds; 1 brood per year

Eggs: 8-10; olive gray to brown without markings

Incubation: 26-27 days; female incubates

Fledging: 49-56 days; female teaches young to feed

Migration: complete, to Florida, other southern states

Food: aquatic plants and insects

Compare: Female Lesser Scaup (pg. 169) is similar in size. Look for the white ring around the bill of the female Ring-necked Duck.

Stan's Notes: One of the most abundant wintering ducks in the state. Usually seen in larger freshwater lakes rather than saltwater marshes. A diving duck, watch for it to dive underwater to forage for food. Takes to flight by springing up off water. Named "Ring-necked" because of the cinnamon collar (nearly impossible to see in the field). Also called Ring-billed Duck due to the white ring on its bill, and Blue Bill by duck hunters.

male pg. 55

female

YEAR-ROUND
WINTER

Hooded Merganser
Lophodytes cucullatus

Size: 16-19" (40-48 cm)

Female: Sleek brown and rust bird with a red head. Ragged "hair" on back of head. Long, thin brown bill.

Male: same size and shape as female, but a black back and rust sides, crest "hood" raises to reveal large white patch, long black bill

Juvenile: similar to female

Nest: cavity; female lines old woodpecker hole; 1 brood per year

Eggs: 10-12; white without markings

Incubation: 32-33 days; female incubates

Fledging: 71 days; female feeds young

Migration: complete to non-migrator in Florida

Food: small fish, aquatic insects

Compare: Female Red-breasted Merganser (pg. 195) is very similar, but is larger and has a larger, lighter bill. Female Lesser Scaup (pg. 169) is smaller and has a dull white patch at the base of its bill.

Stan's Notes: A small diving bird of shallow ponds, sloughs, lakes and rivers. Male Hooded Merganser can voluntarily raise and lower its crest to show off the large white head patch. Rarely found away from wooded areas, where it nests in natural cavities or nest boxes. Female will "dump" her eggs into other female Hooded Merganser nests, resulting in 20-25 eggs in some nests. Known to share nest cavities with Wood Ducks, sitting side by side.

O Tof World
pond

Marbled Godwit
Limosa fedoa

MIGRATION
WINTER

Size: 18" (45 cm)

Male: A tawny brown overall with a darker back. Long, two-toned and slightly upturned bill with black tip and pinkish base. Long gray legs. Cinnamon under wings, seen in flight.

Female: same as male

Juvenile: similar to adult

Nest: ground; female and male construct; 1 brood per year

Eggs: 3-5; olive green with dark markings

Incubation: 21-23 days; male and female incubate

Fledging: 20-21 days; female and male feed young

Migration: complete, to coastal Florida

Food: aquatic insects, snails, worms, leeches

Compare: Larger than the breeding Willet (pg. 165). Same size as Whimbrel (pg. 179), which has a down-curved bill, compared with the slightly upturned bill of the Godwit. Larger than the more common breeding Short-billed Dowitcher (pg. 145), which has a straight black bill.

Stan's Notes: A winter resident that is easily identified by its very long, two-toned, slightly upturned bill. Uses its bill to probe deep into sand and mud for insects. Usually feeds in mid-thigh water. In the winter, prefers saltwater beaches and mud flats up and down the East coast. Returns to Prairie Pothole regions of North Dakota and Canada for nesting. Nests in short grass prairie near wetlands. Name comes from its "godWHIT-godWHIT" call.

Dec 2006,
Dunedin Causeway

Whimbrel

Numenius phaeopus

MIGRATION
WINTER

Size: 18" (45 cm)

Male: Heavily streaked bird, light brown to gray. A long down-curved bill and multiple dark brown stripes on crown. Dark line through eyes. Legs are light gray to blue.

Female: same as male

Juvenile: similar to adult

Nest: ground; female and male construct; 1 brood per year

Eggs: 3-4; olive green with dark markings

Incubation: 27-28 days; male and female incubate

Fledging: 35-42 days; female and male feed young

Migration: complete, to coastal Florida

Food: insects, snails, worms, leeches, berries

Compare: The breeding Willet (pg. 165) lacks a crown with brown stripes and long down-curved bill. Marbled Godwit (pg. 177) is the same size and has an upturned bill. Short-billed Dowitcher (pg. 145) is more common and has a straight black bill. Greater Yellowlegs (pg. 161) is smaller and has yellow legs.

Stan's Notes: A winter resident, easily identified by its very long down-curved bill and brown stripes on head. Uses its bill to probe deep into sand and mud for insects. Unlike the other shorebirds, berries become an important food source in summer. Is very vocal, giving single note whistles. Returns to tundra of northern Alaska to nest. Doesn't breed until age 3. Has a long-term pair bond. Adults leave breeding grounds up to two weeks before the young leave.

male pg. 273

female

YEAR-ROUND
WINTER

Wood Duck
Aix sponsa

Size: 17-20" (43-50 cm)

Female: A small brown dabbling duck. Bright white eye-ring and a not-so-obvious crest. A blue patch on wing, often hidden.

Male: highly ornamented with a green head and crest patterned with white and black, rusty chest, white belly and red eyes

Juvenile: same as female

Nest: cavity; female lines old woodpecker cavity; 1 brood per year

Eggs: 10-15; creamy white without markings

Incubation: 28-36 days; female incubates

Fledging: 56-68 days; female teaches young to feed

Migration: non-migrator to partial in Florida

Food: aquatic insects, plants, seeds

Compare: Female Mallard (pg. 199) and female Blue-winged Teal (pg. 167) lack the bright white eye-ring and crest. The female Northern Shoveler (pg. 183) is larger and has a large spoon-shaped bill.

Stan's Notes: A common duck of quiet, shallow backwater ponds. Nests in old woodpecker holes or in nest boxes. Often seen flying deep in forests or perched high on tree branches. Female takes to flight with a loud squealing call, entering nest cavity from full flight. Will lay eggs in a neighboring female nest (egg dumping), resulting in some clutches in excess of 20 eggs. Young stay in nest cavity only 24 hours after hatching, then jump from up to 30 feet (9 m) to the ground or water to follow their mother, never returning to the nest.

 CD 2, TRACK 19

male pg. 277

female

Northern Shoveler
Anas clypeata

Size: 20" (50 cm)

Female: Medium-sized brown duck speckled with black. Blue wing patch. An extraordinarily large spoon-shaped bill, almost always held pointed toward the water.

Male: iridescent green head, rusty sides and white breast, spoon-shaped bill

Juvenile: same as female

Nest: ground; female builds; 1 brood per year

Eggs: 9-12; olive without markings

Incubation: 22-25 days; female incubates

Fledging: 30-60 days; female leads young to food

Migration: complete, to Florida, other southern states, Mexico and Central America

Food: aquatic insects, plants

Compare: Similar color as female Mallard (pg. 199), but Mallard lacks the Shoveler's large bill. Female Wood Duck (pg. 181) is smaller and has a white eye-ring. Look for the Shoveler's large spoon-shaped bill to help identify.

Stan's Notes: One of several species of shoveler, so called because of the peculiar shape of its bill. The Northern Shoveler is the only species of these ducks in North America. Found in small flocks of 5-10, swimming low in water with its large bill pointed toward the water, as if it's too heavy to lift. Feeds mainly by filtering tiny aquatic insects and plants from the water's surface with its bill. This winter visitor arrives in Florida in September and leaves in April.

Jon 2007   Tierra Verde pond

Mottled Duck
Anas fulvigula

YEAR-ROUND

Size: 22" (56 cm)

Male: All-brown duck with a light tan neck and head. Bright yellow bill without markings. Wing patch (speculum) is blue (sometimes green) and outlined with black.

Female: same as male

Juvenile: same as adult

Nest: ground; female builds; 1 brood per year

Eggs: 5-10; off-white without markings

Incubation: 25-27 days; female incubates

Fledging: 60-70 days; female shows the young what to eat

Migration: non-migrator in Florida

Food: aquatic insects, crayfish, snails, grass, seeds

Compare: Similar to female Mallard (pg. 199), which has an orange bill with black markings. The female Mallard's blue speculum is outlined with white.

Stan's Notes: A year-round resident and widely hunted in Florida. It is most densely populated around the coast in both freshwater and saltwater marshes. Feeds on more insects and crayfish than the Mallard. Will breed with Mallards, producing hybrids. Mated pairs stay together all year, unlike Mallards. Young will scatter if mother feels threatened and gives an alarm call.

soaring

Red-tailed Hawk
Buteo jamaicensis

YEAR-ROUND
WINTER

Size:	19-25" (48-63 cm); up to 4-foot wingspan
Male:	Large hawk with amazing variety of colors from bird to bird, from chocolate brown to nearly all white. Often brown with a white breast and a distinctive brown belly band. Rust red tail, usually seen only from above. Wing underside is white with a small dark patch on leading edge near shoulder.
Female:	same as male, only slightly larger
Juvenile:	similar to adults, lacking the red tail, has a speckled chest and light eyes
Nest:	platform; male and female build; 1 brood per year
Eggs:	2-3; white without markings or sometimes marked with brown
Incubation:	30-35 days; female and male incubate
Fledging:	45-46 days; male and female feed young
Migration:	non-migrator to partial
Food:	mice, birds, snakes, insects, mammals
Compare:	Red-shouldered Hawk (pg. 171) and Sharp-shinned Hawk (pg. 249) are much smaller.

Stan's Notes: A common hawk of open country and in cities, often seen perched on freeway light posts, fences and trees. Look for it circling over open fields and roadsides, searching for prey. Their large stick nests are commonly seen in large trees along roads. Nests are lined with finer material such as evergreen tree needles. Returns to the same nest site each year. Develops red tail in the second year.

Countryside Golf Centre

Barred Owl
Strix varia

YEAR-ROUND

Size: 20-24" (50-60 cm); up to 3½-foot wingspan

Male: A chunky brown and gray owl with a large head and dark brown eyes. Dark horizontal barring on upper chest. Vertical streaks on lower chest and belly. Yellow bill and feet.

Female: same as male, only slightly larger

Juvenile: light gray with a black face

Nest: cavity; does not add any nesting material; 1 brood per year

Eggs: 2-3; white without markings

Incubation: 28-33 days; female incubates

Fledging: 42-44 days; female and male feed young

Migration: non-migrator

Food: mammals, birds, fish, reptiles, amphibians

Compare: Lacks the "horns" of the Great Horned Owl (pg. 191) and ear tufts of the tiny Eastern Screech-Owl (pg. 237). Burrowing Owl (pg. 139) has long legs and is less than half the size of the Barred Owl.

Stan's Notes: A very common owl that can often be seen hunting during the day, perching and watching for mice, birds and other prey. One of the few owls to take fish out of a lake. Prefers dense deciduous woodlands with sparse undergrowth. Can be attracted with a simple nest box with a large opening, attached to a tree. The young stay with their parents for up to four months after fledging. Often sounds like a dog barking just before giving an eight-hoot call that sounds like, "Who-cooks-for-you? Who-cooks-for-you?" The Great Horned Owl sounds like, "Hoo-hoo-hoo-hoooo!"

YEAR-ROUND

Great Horned Owl
Bubo virginianus

Size: 20-25" (50-63 cm); up to 3½-foot wingspan

Male: Robust brown "horned" owl. Bright yellow eyes and V-shaped white throat resembling a necklace. Horizontal barring on the chest.

Female: same as male, only slightly larger

Juvenile: similar to adults, lacking ear tufts

Nest: no nest; takes over the nests of crows, Great Blue Herons and hawks or will use partial cavities, stumps or broken-off trees; 1 brood per year

Eggs: 2; white without markings

Incubation: 26-30 days; female incubates

Fledging: 30-35 days; male and female feed young

Migration: non-migrator

Food: mammals, birds (ducks), snakes, insects

Compare: Burrowing Owl (pg. 139) is much smaller and has long legs. Barred Owl (pg. 189) has dark eyes and lacks "horns." Look for the yellow eyes and feathers on head that look like horns to help identify Great Horned.

Stan's Notes: The largest owl and a winter nester in Florida, laying eggs in January and February. Has excellent hearing; able to hear a mouse move under a foot of snow. "Ears" are tufts of feathers (horns) and have nothing to do with hearing. Not able to turn its head all the way around. Wing feathers are ragged on ends, resulting in silent flight. Eyelids close from the top down, like humans. Fearless, it is one of the few animals that will kill skunks and porcupines. Because of this, it is sometimes called Flying Tiger.

winter

breeding

YEAR-ROUND
MIGRATION

Glossy Ibis
Plegadis falcinellus

Size: 23" (58 cm); up to 3-foot wingspan

Male: Breeding has a chestnut brown head and neck. Iridescent green and blue wings and tail. Appears to be all dark brown from a distance. Very long, down-curved bill with blue facial skin near base. Winter is overall dark with a speckled head.

Female: same as male

Juvenile: same as adult, but lacks iridescent coloring

Nest: platform; female and male build; 1 brood per year

Eggs: 2-4; light blue without markings

Incubation: 20-21 days; female and male incubate

Fledging: 28-32 days; female and male feed young

Migration: partial to non-migrator in Florida

Food: aquatic insects, crustaceans

Compare: The long, down-curved bill helps identify the ibis. The Glossy Ibis is brown and not to be confused with the adult White Ibis (pg. 315), which is all white.

Stan's Notes: One of two native ibis species in Florida. Seems to be on the increase in the state. Prefers fresh water over salt water, with crayfish a big part of its diet. From a distance the Glossy Ibis appears dark brown or nearly black, but when seen up close or through binoculars its iridescent green and bluish purple colors are amazing. Its long down-curved bill helps identify it in flight. Often seen flying in groups of 30 or more. Nests in large colonies with other wading birds.

male pg. 279

female

MIGRATION
WINTER

Red-breasted Merganser
Mergus serrator

Size: 23" (58 cm)

Female: Overall brown-to-gray duck with a shaggy reddish head and crest. Long orange bill.

Male: shaggy green head and crest, a prominent white collar, rusty breast, black and white body, long orange bill

Juvenile: similar to female

Nest: ground; female builds; 1 brood per year

Eggs: 5-10; olive green without markings

Incubation: 29-30 days; female incubates

Fledging: 55-65 days; female feeds young

Migration: complete, to coastal Florida

Food: fish, aquatic insects

Compare: The female Hooded Merganser (pg. 175) is very similar, but smaller and has a smaller, darker bill.

Stan's Notes: A winter resident in coastal Florida. This is the most common of the wintering mergansers, arriving in late October and leaving in April. Most commonly seen along the Florida coast, but can also be seen in large inland freshwater lakes. A very fast flier, clocked at up to 100 miles (161 km) per hour. Often seen flying low across the water. Needs a long run for takeoff with wings flapping to get airborne. Serrated bill helps it catch slippery fish. Usually is a silent duck. Male sometimes gives a soft, catlike meow. Female gives a harsh "krrr-croak." Doesn't breed before 2 years of age. The male will abandon the female just after eggs are laid. Females often share nests. Breeds across Alaska and northern Canada. The young leave the nest within 24 hours of hatching, never to return.

male pg. 257

female

soaring

Northern Harrier
Circus cyaneus

WINTER

Size: 22-24" (56-60 cm); up to 3½-foot wingspan

Female: A slim, low-flying hawk. Dark brown back with brown-streaked breast and belly. Large white rump patch and narrow black bands across tail. Black wing tips. Yellow eyes.

Male: silver gray with large white rump patch and white belly, faint narrow bands across tail, black wing tips, yellow eyes

Juvenile: similar to female, with an orange breast

Nest: platform, often on ground; female and male build; 1 brood per year

Eggs: 4-8; bluish white without markings

Incubation: 31-32 days; female incubates

Fledging: 30-35 days; male and female feed young

Migration: complete, to Florida, other southern states, Mexico and Central America

Food: mice, snakes, insects, small birds

Compare: Slimmer than Red-tailed Hawk (pg. 187). Look for black tail bands, white rump patch and characteristic flight to help identify.

Stan's Notes: One of the easiest hawks to identify. Harriers glide just above ground, following contours of the land while searching for prey. Holds its wings just above the horizontal position, tilting back and forth in the wind, similar to Turkey Vultures. Formerly called Marsh Hawk due to its habit of hunting over marshes. Feeds on the ground. Will perch on the ground to preen and rest. At any age, has a distinctive owl-like face disk.

 CD 2, TRACK 27

197

female

male pg. 281

YEAR-ROUND

Mallard
Anas platyrhynchos

Size: 20-28" (50-71 cm)

Female: Brown duck with an orange and black bill and blue and white wing mark (speculum).

Male: large, bulbous green head, white necklace, rust brown or chestnut chest, combination of gray and white on the sides, yellow bill, orange legs and feet

Juvenile: same as female, but with a yellow bill

Nest: ground; female builds; 1 brood per year

Eggs: 7-10; greenish to whitish, unmarked

Incubation: 26-30 days; female incubates

Fledging: 42-52 days; female leads young to food

Migration: non-migrator in Florida

Food: seeds, plants, aquatic insects; will come to ground feeders offering corn

Compare: Mottled Duck (pg. 185) is similar, but has a yellow bill. Female Shoveler (pg. 183) is smaller and has a large spoon-shaped bill. The female Wood Duck (pg. 181) has a white eye-ring. Female Blue-winged Teal (pg. 167) is smaller than female Mallard.

Stan's Notes: A familiar duck of lakes and ponds, it's considered a type of dabbling duck, tipping forward in shallow water to feed on aquatic plants on the bottom. The name "Mallard" comes from the Latin *masculus*, meaning "male," referring to the habit of males not taking part in raising ducklings. Both female and male have white tails and white underwings. Black central tail feathers of male curl upward. Will return to place of birth.

Common   Florida

 CD 2, TRACK 28

Wild Turkey
Meleagris gallopavo

Size: 36-48" (90-120 cm)

Male: Large, plump brown and bronze bird with a striking blue and red bare head. Fan tail and a long, straight black beard in center of chest. Spurs on legs.

Female: thinner and less striking than male, usually lacking a breast beard

Juvenile: same as adult of the same sex

Nest: ground; female builds; 1 brood per year

Eggs: 10-12; buff white with dull brown markings

Incubation: 27-28 days; female incubates

Fledging: 6-10 days; female leads young to food

Migration: non-migrator

Food: insects, seeds, fruit

Compare: This bird is quite distinctive and unlikely to be confused with others.

Stan's Notes: The largest native game bird in Florida, and the bird from which the domestic turkey was bred. It almost became our national bird, losing to the Bald Eagle by one vote. Eliminated from many of the eastern states due to market hunting and the loss of habitat. Reintroduced widely in the 1960-80s. Populations are now stable. A strong flier that can approach 60 miles (97 km) per hour. Can fly straight up, then away. Eyesight is three times better than in humans. Hearing is excellent; able to hear competing males up to a mile away. Males hold "harems" of up to 20 females. Males are known as toms, females are hens, young are called poults. Roosts in trees at night.

juvenile

breeding

chick-feeding adult

YEAR-ROUND

Brown Pelican
Pelecanus occidentalis

Size: 48" (120 cm); up to 9-foot wingspan

Male: Gray brown body, black belly, exceptionally long gray bill. Breeding adult has a white or yellow head with dark chestnut hind neck. Adult that is feeding chicks (chick-feeding adult) has a speckled white head. A non-breeding adult has a white head and neck.

Female: similar to male

Juvenile: brown with white breast and belly, does not acquire adult plumage until third year

Nest: platform; female and male build; 1 brood per year

Eggs: 2-4; white without markings

Incubation: 28-30 days; female and male incubate

Fledging: 71-86 days; female and male feed young

Migration: non-migrator along coastal Florida

Food: fish

Compare: An unmistakable bird in Florida.

Stan's Notes: A common bird of Florida, although it was recently an endangered species. Suffering from eggshell thinning in the 1970s due to DDT and other pesticides, the only population that remained viable was in Florida. It is now reestablishing along the East, Gulf and West coasts. Captures fish by diving headfirst into the ocean, opening its large bill and "netting" fish with its gular pouch. Often seen sitting on posts around marinas. Nests in large colonies. Does not breed before the age of 3, when it obtains its breeding plumage.

common Florida

Ruby-crowned Kinglet
Regulus calendula

WINTER

Size: 4" (10 cm)

Male: Small, teardrop-shaped green-to-gray bird with 2 white wing bars and a hidden ruby crown. White eye-ring.

Female: same as male, but lacking the ruby crown

Juvenile: same as female

Nest: pendulous; female builds; 1 brood per year

Eggs: 4-5; white with brown markings

Incubation: 11-12 days; female incubates

Fledging: 11-12 days; female and male feed young

Migration: complete, to Florida, other southern states, Mexico and Central America

Food: insects, berries

Compare: The female American Goldfinch (pg. 323) is larger, but shares the same olive color and unmarked breast. Look for the white eye-ring of Ruby-crowned Kinglet.

Stan's Notes: One of the smaller birds in Florida. Most commonly seen during migration. Look for it flitting around thick shrubs low to the ground. It takes a quick eye to see the male's ruby crown. Female builds an unusual pendulous (sac-like) nest, intricately woven and decorated on the outside with colored lichens and mosses stuck together with spider webs. The nest is suspended from a branch overlapped by leaves and usually is hung high in a mature tree. The common name "Kinglet" comes from the Anglo-Saxon word *cyning*, or "king," referring to the male's ruby crown, and the diminutive suffix "let," meaning "small."

YEAR-ROUND

Brown-headed Nuthatch
Sitta pusilla

Size: 4½" (11 cm)

Male: Gray back. Brown cap bordered by a black line that extends through eyes. A dull white chin, breast and belly. Pale gray spot at the nape of neck, hard to see from a distance.

Female: same as male

Juvenile: same as adult

Nest: cavity; female and male construct; 1 brood per year

Eggs: 3-5; white with dark markings

Incubation: 12-14 days; female incubates

Fledging: 18-19 days; female and male feed young

Migration: non-migrator

Food: insects, seeds; comes to seed feeders

Compare: Carolina Chickadee (pg. 209) is similar in size, but has a black cap unlike the brown cap of the Brown-headed Nuthatch.

Stan's Notes: A tiny bird of open pine forest in Florida. Like other nuthatches, it feeds by creeping up and down twigs and trunks of trees, looking for insects and insect eggs. Works hard to remove seeds from cones on evergreen trees. Has been known to cache pine seeds for later consumption. Will visit seed feeders. A cavity nester, it excavates a cavity, takes an abandoned woodpecker home or uses a nest box. Occasionally an unmated male helper attends to a mated female on the nest. Will stay with mate nearly all year, defending a very small territory.

 CD 2, TRACK 32

YEAR-ROUND

Carolina Chickadee
Poecile carolinensis

Size: 5" (13 cm)

Male: Mostly gray bird with a black cap and chin. White face and chest with tan belly. Darker gray tail.

Female: same as male

Juvenile: same as adult

Nest: cavity; female and male build or excavate; 1-2 broods per year

Eggs: 5-7; white with reddish brown markings

Incubation: 11-12 days; female and male incubate

Fledging: 13-17 days; female and male feed young

Migration: non-migrator

Food: insects, seeds, fruit; comes to seed and suet feeders

Compare: Similar in size to Brown-headed Nuthatch (pg. 207), but lacks the brown cap. Tufted Titmouse (pg. 213) is a close relative, but has an erect crest and lacks the black cap and chin.

Stan's Notes: A common year-round bird of Florida. One of the first birds to use a newly placed feeder. Flies to a feeder, grabs a seed and carries it to a branch. To get to the meat inside, holds the seed down with its feet and hammers the shell open with its bill. Returns for another seed. A friendly bird. Can be tamed and hand fed. Attracted with a nest box that has a 1¼-inch (3 cm) entrance hole. Female will give a loud snake-like hiss when disturbed on the nest. Often seen with other birds (mixed flock) in winter. Song is a high, fast "chika-dee-dee-dee-dee."

male

first winter

female

WINTER

Yellow-rumped Warbler
Dendroica coronata

Size: 5-6" (13-15 cm)

Male: Slate gray bird with black streaks on breast. Yellow patches on rump, flanks and head. White chin and belly. Two white wing bars.

Female: duller than male, but same yellow patches

Juvenile: similar to female

Nest: cup; female builds; 2 broods per year

Eggs: 4-5; white with brown markings

Incubation: 12-13 days; female incubates

Fledging: 10-12 days; female and male feed young

Migration: complete, to Florida, other southern states, Mexico and Central America

Food: insects, berries; rarely comes to suet feeders

Compare: Male Common Yellowthroat (pg. 325) has a yellow breast and a very distinctive black mask. The Palm Warbler (pg. 327) has a yellow throat and chestnut cap. Look for a combination of yellow patches on the rump, flanks and head of Yellow-rumped Warbler.

Stan's Notes: This is one of our most common winter warblers. Male molts to a dull color in winter similar to the female, retaining the yellow patches. Often called Myrtle Warbler in eastern states and Audubon's Warbler in western states. Sometimes called Butter-butts due to the yellow patch on its rump. Familiar call is a single robust "chip," heard mostly during migration. This species also has a wonderful song in spring.

common

Florida

Tufted Titmouse
Baeolophus bicolor

YEAR-ROUND

Size: 6" (15 cm)

Male: Slate gray bird with a white chest and belly. Pointed crest. Flanks are washed in a rusty brown. Gray legs and dark eyes.

Female: same as male

Juvenile: same as adult

Nest: cavity; female lines old woodpecker hole; 2 broods per year

Eggs: 5-7; white with brown markings

Incubation: 13-14 days; female incubates

Fledging: 15-18 days; female and male feed young

Migration: non-migrator

Food: insects, seeds, fruit; will come to seed and suet feeders

Compare: Closely related to the slightly smaller Carolina Chickadee (pg. 209), but Tufted Titmouse has a crest. Larger than Brown-headed Nuthatch (pg. 207) and lacks the brown cap of the Nuthatch.

Stan's Notes: A common feeder bird, it can be attracted with black oil sunflower seeds. Well known for its quickly repeated "peter-peter-peter" call. Prefix "Tit" comes from a Scandinavian word meaning "little." Suffix "mouse" is derived from the Old English word *mase*, meaning "bird." Simply translated, it is a "small bird." Notorious for pulling hair from sleeping dogs, cats and squirrels to line their nests. Attracted with nest boxes. Usually seen only one or two at a time. Male feeds female during courtship and nesting.

N. Carolina
I-81 N
Jan. 29 2007

breeding
pg. 115

winter

MIGRATION
WINTER

Least Sandpiper
Calidris minutilla

Size: 6" (15 cm)

Male: Overall gray to light brown winter plumage with a distinct brown breast band and light gray eyebrows. White belly and dull yellow legs. Short, down-curved black bill.

Female: same as male

Juvenile: similar to winter adult, but buff brown and lacks the breast band

Nest: ground; male and female construct; 1 brood per year

Eggs: 3-4; olive with dark markings

Incubation: 19-23 days; male and female incubate

Fledging: 25-28 days; male and female feed young

Migration: complete, to coastal Florida

Food: aquatic and terrestrial insects, seeds

Compare: The smallest of sandpipers. Often confused with winter Western Sandpiper (pg. 219) and Semipalmated Sandpiper (pg. 217), Least Sandpiper's yellow legs differentiate it from other tiny sandpipers. The short, thin, down-curved bill also helps to identify.

Stan's Notes: A winter resident in coastal Florida. Also winters in other coastal states from the Carolinas to California. This is a tiny, tame sandpiper that can be approached without scaring. It is the smallest of peeps (sandpipers), nesting on the tundra in northern regions of Canada and Alaska. Prefers grassy flats of saltwater and freshwater ponds. Its yellow legs can be difficult to see in water, poor light or when covered with mud.

 CD 1, TRACK 55   *Fort de Soto Park*

breeding

winter

Semipalmated Sandpiper
Calidris pusilla

MIGRATION

Size: 6" (15 cm)

Male: Plump gray shorebird. Winter plumage has a grayish brown head, neck and back and a white chest and eyebrows. Black legs. Short, straight, blunt-tipped black bill. Breeding plumage (usually seen in the Arctic) has a brown head, some black and brown spots on the back and a white belly.

Female: same as male

Juvenile: overall gray brown with black spots

Nest: ground; male and female construct; 1 brood per year

Eggs: 2-4; light yellow with brown markings

Incubation: 18-22 days; male and female incubate

Fledging: 18-20 days; male and female feed young

Migration: complete, to Bahamas and northern South America

Food: aquatic insects

Compare: Much smaller and darker gray than winter Sanderling (pg. 229).

Stan's Notes: The most common shorebird in Florida, seen during migration in spring (mid-May to early June) and autumn (July to August). Few individuals remain year-round. The male does most of the care of the young after hatching, since the female abandons her family approximately 2-3 days after the eggs hatch. Retains the same mate for several years. Nests in northern Canada and Alaska.

breeding
pg. 117

winter

Western Sandpiper
Calidris mauri

Size: 6½" (16 cm)

Male: Winter plumage is dull gray to light brown overall with a white belly and eyebrows. Black legs. Narrow bill that droops near tip.

Female: same as male

Juvenile: similar to breeding adult, bright buff brown on the back only

Nest: ground; male and female construct; 1 brood per year

Eggs: 2-4; light brown with dark markings

Incubation: 20-22 days; male and female incubate

Fledging: 19-21 days; male and female feed young

Migration: complete, to coastal Florida

Food: aquatic and terrestrial insects

Compare: The winter Least Sandpiper (pg. 215) and Semipalmated Sandpiper (pg. 217) are very similar, but the Least Sandpiper lacks black legs. The Western Sandpiper has a longer bill that droops slightly at the tip.

Stan's Notes: A winter resident in coastal Florida. Also winters in other coastal states from the Carolinas to California. Nests on the ground in large "loose" colonies on the tundra of northern coastal Alaska. Adults leave the breeding grounds several weeks before the young. Some obtain breeding plumage before leaving the state in spring. Feeds on insects at the water's edge, sometimes immersing its head. Will feed in deeper water than Semipalmated Sandpipers. Young leave the nest (precocial) within a few hours after hatching. Female leaves and the male tends the hatchlings.

 CD 1, TRACK 56

Common Ground-Dove
Columbina passerina

YEAR-ROUND

Size: 6½" (16 cm)

Male: A very small dove with a short tail and a unique scalloped appearance on head and chest. Black-tipped reddish orange bill and slate gray crown. Pinkish gray underside. Bright chestnut wing linings, seen in flight.

Female: similar to male, but grayer and has a more uniform color

Juvenile: similar to adult

Nest: ground; female and male build; 2-4 broods per year

Eggs: 2-4; white without markings

Incubation: 12-14 days; female and male incubate

Fledging: 10-11 days; female and male feed young

Migration: non-migrator

Food: seeds, berries; will come to seed feeders

Compare: The Mourning Dove (pg. 155) is twice the size of Common Ground-Dove, lacks the scalloped appearance and chestnut-colored wing linings.

Stan's Notes: The smallest dove in Florida, formerly called Eastern Ground Dove. Known to continually bob its head. Frequently seen in pairs. Unafraid of humans and spends most of its time on the ground. While it usually nests on the ground, it sometimes builds a flimsy nest in a shrub or takes an abandoned nest low in a tree. Seen in open dry woodlands, old fields and pastures. Walks around with mechanical movements, bobbing its head and shuffling its feet like a wind-up toy.

Eastern Phoebe
Sayornis phoebe

WINTER

Size: 7" (18 cm)

Male: Gray bird with dark wings, light olive green belly and a thin dark bill.

Female: same as male

Juvenile: same as adult

Nest: cup; female builds; 2 broods per year

Eggs: 4-5; white without markings

Incubation: 15-16 days; female incubates

Fledging: 15-16 days; male and female feed young

Migration: complete, to Florida, other southern states and Mexico

Food: insects

Compare: Like most other olive gray birds, it is hard to distinguish identifying markings. Eastern Phoebe lacks any white eye-ring. Easier to identify by well-enunciated song, "fee-bee," or characteristic of hawking for insects.

Stan's Notes: A sparrow-sized bird often seen on the end of a dead branch. It sits in wait for a passing insect, flies out to catch it, then returns to the same branch, a process called hawking. Has a habit of pumping its tail up and down and spreading it when perched. Will build its nest under the eaves of a house, under a bridge or in culverts. Nest is constructed with mud, grass and moss, and lined with hair (and sometimes feathers). The name is derived from its characteristic song, "fee-bee," which is repeated over and over from the tops of dead branches.

Eastern Kingbird
Tyrannus tyrannus

SUMMER

Size: 8" (20 cm)

Male: Mostly black gray bird with white belly and chin. Black head and tail with a distinctive white band across the end of the tail. Has a concealed red crown that is rarely seen.

Female: same as male

Juvenile: same as adult

Nest: cup; male and female construct; 1 brood per year

Eggs: 3-4; white with brown markings

Incubation: 16-18 days; female incubates

Fledging: 16-18 days; female and male feed young

Migration: complete, to Mexico, Central America and South America

Food: insects, fruit

Compare: Medium-sized bird, smaller than American Robin (pg. 239). Eastern Phoebe (pg. 223) is smaller and lacks Kingbird's white belly. Look for a white band on the Kingbird's tail.

Stan's Notes: A summer resident seen in open fields and pastures. Up to 20 individuals will migrate together in a group. Returns to the mating ground in spring, where male and female defend their territory. Acting unafraid of other birds and chasing the larger ones, it is perceived as having an attitude. Its bold behavior gave rise to the common name, King. Perches on tall branches and watches for insects. After flying out to catch them, returns to the same perch, a technique called hawking. Becomes very vocal during late summer, when entire families call back and forth while hunting for insects.

Great Crested Flycatcher
Myiarchus crinitus

Size: 8" (20 cm)

Male: Gray head with prominent crest. Gray back and throat with bright yellow belly, yellow extending under reddish brown tail. Lower bill is yellow at base.

Female: same as male

Juvenile: same as adult

Nest: cavity; female and male construct; 1 brood per year

Eggs: 4-6; white or buff with brown markings

Incubation: 13-15 days; female incubates

Fledging: 14-21 days; female and male feed young

Migration: complete to non-migrator in Florida

Food: insects, fruit

Compare: The Eastern Kingbird (pg. 225) has a white band across the tail. Similar to the Eastern Phoebe (pg. 223), but the Great Crested Flycatcher has a crest and yellow belly.

Stan's Notes: A common bird of wooded areas in Florida. It lives high up in trees, rarely coming to ground. Often heard before seen. The first part of its common name refers to the set of extra long feathers on top of its head (crest), which the bird raises when alert or agitated, like the Northern Cardinal. Feeds by gleaning insects from tree leaves. Nests in former woodpecker holes, but can be attracted to a nest box with a 1½-2½-inch (4-6 cm) entrance hole placed high in a tree. Frequently stuffs its nest with a collection of fur, feathers, string and snakeskins. Breeds throughout the state.

Countryside Golf Centre
Jan - 2007

breeding
pg. 129

winter

Sanderling
Calidris alba

Size: 8" (20 cm)

Male: The lightest sandpiper on the beach during winter. Winter plumage head and back are gray and belly is white. Black legs and bill. White wing stripe, seen only in flight.

Female: same as male

Juvenile: spotty black on the head and back, a white belly, black legs and bill

Nest: ground; male builds; 1-2 broods per year

Eggs: 3-4; greenish olive with brown markings

Incubation: 24-30 days; male and female incubate

Fledging: 16-17 days; female and male feed young

Migration: complete, to coastal Florida, other southern coastal states, Mexico and Central America

Food: insects

Compare: The winter Black-bellied Plover (pg. 247) is much larger with a larger bill.

MIGRATION
WINTER

Stan's Notes: One of the most common shorebirds in the state, but mostly seen in its gray winter plumage from August to April. Can be seen in groups on sandy beaches, running out with each retreating wave to feed. Look for a flash of white on wings when it's in flight. Sometimes a female mates with several males (polyandry), which results in males and the female incubating separate nests. Both sexes perform a distraction display when threatened. Nests on the Arctic tundra. Rests while standing on one leg (see inset) and tucking the other leg into its belly feathers. Often hops away on one leg, moving away from pedestrians on the beach. Surveys show a greater than 80 percent decline in numbers since the 1970s.

CD 1, TRACK 60   common Beaches

breeding
pg. 131

winter

Dunlin
Calidris alpina

MIGRATION
WINTER

Size: 8-9" (20-22.5 cm)

Male: Winter adult has a brownish gray back with a light gray chest and white belly. Stout bill curves slightly downward at tip. Black legs.

Female: slightly larger than male, with a longer bill

Juvenile: slightly rusty back with a spotty chest

Nest: ground; male and female construct; 1 brood per year

Eggs: 2-4; olive buff or blue green with red brown markings

Incubation: 21-22 days; male and female incubate, male incubates during the day, female at night

Fledging: 19-21 days; male feeds young, female often leaves before young fledge

Migration: complete, to coastal Florida, other southern coastal states, Mexico and Central America

Food: insects

Compare: Similar size as winter Sanderling (pg. 229), but the winter Dunlin has a longer down-turned bill and is an overall darker gray.

Stan's Notes: Usually seen in gray winter plumage from August to early May. Breeding plumage is more commonly seen in the spring. Flights include heights of up to 100 feet (30 m) with brief gliding alternating with shallow flutters, and a rhythmic, repeating song. Huge flocks fly synchronously, with birds twisting and turning, flashing light and dark undersides. Males tend to fly farther south in winter than females. Winter visitor along the coast. Doesn't nest in Florida.

CD 1, TRACK 61

Gray Catbird
Dumetella carolinensis

Size: 9" (22.5 cm)

Male: Handsome slate gray bird with black crown and a long, thin black bill. Often seen with its tail lifted up, exposing a chestnut patch under the tail.

Female: same as male

Juvenile: same as adult

Nest: cup; female and male construct; 2 broods per year

Eggs: 4-6; blue green without markings

Incubation: 12-13 days; female incubates

Fledging: 10-11 days; female and male feed young

Migration: complete to non-migrator in Florida

Food: insects, fruit

Compare: Larger than Eastern Phoebe (pg. 223), it lacks the Phoebe's olive belly. Similar size as Eastern Kingbird (pg. 225), but it lacks the Kingbird's white belly and white tail band.

Stan's Notes: A secretive bird that the Chippewa Indians named Bird That Cries With Grief due to its raspy call. The call sounds like the mewing of a house cat, hence the common name. Frequently mimics other birds, rarely repeating the same phrases. More often heard than seen. Nests in thick shrubs and quickly flies back into shrubs if approached. If a cowbird introduces an egg into a catbird nest, the catbird will quickly break it, then eject it.

Jan.
Honeymoon Island

YEAR-ROUND

Loggerhead Shrike
Lanius ludovicianus

Size: 9" (22.5 cm)

Male: A gray head and back with black wings and mask across the eyes. A white chin, breast and belly. Black tail, legs and feet. Black bill with hooked tip. White wing patches, seen in flight.

Female: same as male

Juvenile: dull version of adult

Nest: cup; male and female construct; 1-2 broods per year

Eggs: 4-7; off-white with dark markings

Incubation: 16-17 days; female incubates

Fledging: 17-21 days; female and male feed young

Migration: non-migrator in Florida

Food: insects, lizards, small mammals, frogs

Compare: The Northern Mockingbird (pg. 241) has a similar color pattern, but lacks the black mask. The Cedar Waxwing (pg. 123) has a black mask, but is a brown bird, not gray and black like the Loggerhead Shrike.

Stan's Notes: The Loggerhead is a songbird that acts like a bird of prey. Known for skewering prey on barbed wire fences, thorns and other sharp objects to store or hold still while tearing apart to eat, hence its other common name, Butcher Bird. Feet are too weak to hold the prey it eats. Loggerhead Shrikes from northern states enter Florida during winter, swelling populations. Breeding bird surveys indicate declining populations in the Great Plains due to pesticides killing its major food source—grasshoppers.

CD 2, TRACK 42   *Honeymoon Island*

235

red morph

gray morph

YEAR-ROUND

Eastern Screech-Owl
Megascops asio

Size: 9" (22.5 cm); up to 20-inch wingspan

Male: Small "eared" owl that occurs in one of two permanent color morphs. Is either mottled with gray and white or is red brown (rust) with white. Bright yellow eyes.

Female: same as male

Juvenile: lighter color than adult of the same morph, usually no ear tufts

Nest: cavity, former woodpecker cavity; does not add any nesting material; 1 brood per year

Eggs: 4-5; white without markings

Incubation: 25-26 days; female incubates, male feeds female during incubation

Fledging: 26-27 days; male and female feed young

Migration: non-migrator

Food: large insects, small mammals, birds, snakes

Compare: Burrowing Owl (pg. 139) is slightly larger and lacks ear tufts. Eastern Screech-Owl is hard to confuse with its considerably larger cousin, the Great Horned Owl (pg. 191).

Stan's Notes: A common owl active at dusk and during the night. Excellent hearing and eyesight. Will seldom give a screeching call; more commonly gives a tremulous, descending whiny trill, like a sound effect of a scary movie. Will nest in a wooden nest box. Often seen sunning themselves at nest box holes during the winter. Male and female may roost together at night, and are thought to mate for life. Different colorations are known as morphs. The gray morph is more common than the red.

 CD 2, TRACK 43

male

female

YEAR-ROUND
WINTER

American Robin
Turdus migratorius

Size: 9-11" (22.5-28 cm)

Male: A familiar gray bird with a rusty red breast and nearly black head and tail. White chin with black streaks. White eye-ring.

Female: similar to male, but with a gray head and a duller breast

Juvenile: similar to female, but has a speckled breast and brown back

Nest: cup; female builds with help from the male; 2-3 broods per year

Eggs: 4-7; pale blue without markings

Incubation: 12-14 days; female incubates

Fledging: 14-16 days; female and male feed young

Migration: complete, to Florida, other southern states, Mexico, Central America, small percentage are non-migrators

Food: insects, fruit, berries, earthworms

Compare: Familiar bird to all.

Stan's Notes: A common winter resident in Florida. Can be heard singing all night in spring. Most people don't realize how easy it is to differentiate between the male and female robins. Compare the male's dark, nearly black head and brick red breast with the female's gray head and dull red breast. Robins are not listening for worms when cocking their heads to one side. They are looking with eyes placed far back on the sides of their heads. A very territorial bird. Often seen fighting its own reflection in windows.

Large flocks Jan 2007
eating - feasting on
Brazilian pepper red fruit

displaying

YEAR-ROUND

Northern Mockingbird
Mimus polyglottos

Size: 10" (25 cm)

Male: Silvery gray head and back with light gray chest and belly. White wing patches, seen in flight or during display. Tail mostly black with white outer tail feathers. Black bill.

Female: same as male

Juvenile: dull gray, a heavily streaked chest, gray bill

Nest: cup; female and male build; 2 broods per year, sometimes more

Eggs: 3-5; blue green with brown markings

Incubation: 12-13 days; female incubates

Fledging: 11-13 days; female and male feed young

Migration: non-migrator in Florida

Food: insects, fruit

Compare: Loggerhead Shrike (pg. 235) has a similar color pattern, but is stockier, has a black mask and perches in more open places. The Gray Catbird (pg. 233) is slate gray and lacks wing patches. Look for Mockingbird to spread its wings, flash its white wing patches and wag its tail from side to side.

Stan's Notes: Very animated bird. Performs an elaborate mating dance. Facing each other with heads and tails erect, pairs will run toward each other, flashing white wing patches, and then retreat to cover nearby. Thought to flash wing patches to scare up bugs when hunting. Sits for long periods on top of a shrub. Imitates other birds (vocal mimicry), hence the common name. Young males often sing at night. Often unafraid of people, allowing for close observation.

CD 2, TRACK 45   common   Safety Harbor

White-winged Dove
Zenaida asiatica

YEAR-ROUND
MIGRATION

Size: 11" (28 cm)

Male: Light gray-to-brown dove. A conspicuous white edge on the wings. Small black dash underneath the cheeks. Vivid blue eye-rings around bright red eyes. Black wing tips with a white patch across the middle of wings, as seen in flight.

Female: same as male

Juvenile: similar to adult

Nest: platform; female and male build; 2-3 broods per year

Eggs: 2-4; white without markings

Incubation: 13-14 days; female and male incubate

Fledging: 13-16 days; female and male feed young

Migration: non-migrator to partial

Food: seeds, fruit; will come to seed feeders

Compare: Slightly smaller than the Mourning Dove (pg. 155), which lacks the white line on closed wings and a white and black pattern in flight.

Stan's Notes: Very similar to the Mourning Dove in behavior and appearance. Feeds on the ground, pecking at seeds and tiny grains of rock to aid digestion. Parents feed young a regurgitated liquid called crop-milk the first few days of life. Male uses its white and black wing coloration to display to mate. May nest alone or in large colonies. Year-round resident in most of Florida, but it is not native, being introduced in the 1950s when captive birds were released near Homestead. Gives a distinctive call, "coo-cuk-ca-roo."

breeding
pg. 145

winter

Short-billed Dowitcher
Limnodromus griseus

YEAR-ROUND
MIGRATION

Size: 11" (28 cm)

Male: Winter plumage back and wings are gray to light brown and the belly is white. Has a long, straight black bill. Off-white eyebrow stripe. Dull yellow-to-green legs and feet.

Female: same as male

Juvenile: similar to winter adult

Nest: ground; female and male construct; 1 brood per year

Eggs: 3-4; olive green with dark markings

Incubation: 20-21 days; male and female incubate

Fledging: 25-27 days; male and female feed young

Migration: complete to non-migrator in Florida

Food: insects, snails, worms, leeches, seeds

Compare: The winter Black-bellied Plover (pg. 247) is similar in size, but has a tiny bill compared with the Dowitcher's long bill. Smaller than winter Willet (pg. 255), which has a shorter bill and bold black and white wing linings.

Stan's Notes: A common year-round resident found along coastal Florida and inland on freshwater lakes and marshes. With a rapid probing action like a sewing machine, it uses its long straight bill to probe deep into sand and mud for insects. Can be seen with the less common Long-billed Dowitcher (not shown), but it is difficult to tell the two apart.

Fort De Soto Park

breeding
pg. 47

winter

Black-bellied Plover
Pluvialis squatarola

MIGRATION
WINTER

Size: 11-12" (28-30 cm)

Male: Winter plumage is uniform light gray with dark, nearly black streaks. White belly and chest. Faint white eyebrow mark. Black legs and bill.

Female: less black on belly and breast than male

Juvenile: grayer than adults, with much less black

Nest: ground; male and female construct; 1 brood per year

Eggs: 3-4; pinkish or greenish with black brown markings

Incubation: 26-27 days; male and female incubate, male incubates during the day, female at night

Fledging: 35-45 days; male feeds young, young learn quickly to feed themselves

Migration: complete, to coastal Florida

Food: insects

Compare: Winter Dunlin (pg. 231) has a long down-curved bill. Winter Sanderling (pg. 229) has a smaller bill. Winter Spotted Sandpiper (pg. 127) has a shorter, thicker bill.

Stan's Notes: Males perform a "butterfly" courtship flight to attract females. Female leaves male and young about 12 days after the eggs hatch. Breeds at age 3. A winter resident along the Florida coast. Begins arriving in July and August (fall migration). During flight, in any plumage, displays a white rump and stripe on wings with black axillaries (armpits). Often darts across the ground to grab an insect and run.

Dunedin Causeway

soaring

juvenile

WINTER

Sharp-shinned Hawk
Accipiter striatus

Size: 10-14" (25-36 cm); up to 2-foot wingspan

Male: Small woodland hawk with a gray back and head and a rusty red breast. Long tail with several dark tail bands, widest band at end of squared-off tail. Red eyes.

Female: same as male, only larger

Juvenile: same size as adults, with a brown back and heavily streaked breast, yellow eyes

Nest: platform; female builds; 1 brood per year

Eggs: 4-5; white with brown markings

Incubation: 32-35 days; female incubates

Fledging: 24-27 days; female and male feed young

Migration: complete, to Florida, other southern states, Mexico and Central America

Food: birds, small mammals

Compare: Red-shouldered Hawk (pg. 171) is larger, has a reddish head and belly and lacks the gray back of the Sharp-shinned Hawk.

Stan's Notes: A common hawk of backyards and woodlands, often seen swooping in on birds visiting feeders. Its short rounded wings and long tail allow this hawk to navigate through thick stands of trees in pursuit of prey. Common name comes from the sharp keel on the leading edge of its "shin," though it is actually below rather than above the bird's ankle on the tarsus bone of foot. The tarsus in most birds is round.

Countryside Golf Centre

YEAR-ROUND

Eurasian Collared-Dove
Streptopelia decaocto

Size: 12½" (32 cm)

Male: Head, neck, chest and belly are pale gray to light tan. Slightly darker back, wings and tail. Black collar is bordered with white and extends around nape. Long squared-off tail.

Female: same as male

Juvenile: similar to adult

Nest: platform; female and male construct; 2-3 broods per year

Eggs: 3-5; creamy white without markings

Incubation: 12-14 days; female and male incubate

Fledging: 12-14 days; female and male feed young

Migration: non-migrator

Food: seeds

Compare: Slightly larger and lighter in color than the Mourning Dove (pg. 155). Look for a black collar and squared tail to help identify.

Stan's Notes: A non-native bird that spread to Florida in the early 1980s after being introduced to the Bahamas. Reaching the northern states beginning in the late 1990s, it is expanding throughout North America. Predicted to spread throughout North America in the same way it spread throughout Europe from the Middle East. Nearly identical to Ringed Turtle-Dove, a common pet bird species.

Rock Pigeon
Columba livia

YEAR-ROUND

Size: 13" (33 cm)

Male: No set color pattern. Gray to white, patches of iridescent greens and blues, usually with a light rump patch.

Female: same as male

Juvenile: same as adult

Nest: platform; female builds; 3-4 broods per year

Eggs: 1-2; white without markings

Incubation: 18-20 days; female and male incubate

Fledging: 25-26 days; female and male feed young

Migration: non-migrator

Food: seeds

Compare: Mourning Dove (pg. 155) is smaller, light brown and lacks all the color variations of Rock Pigeon. The Eurasian Collared-Dove (pg. 251) is gray with a black collar.

Stan's Notes: Also known as Domestic Pigeon, formerly known as Rock Dove. Introduced to North America from Europe by the early settlers. This bird is most common around cities and barnyards, where it scratches for seeds. One of the few birds that has a wide variety of colors, produced by years of selective breeding while in captivity. Parents feed their young a regurgitated liquid known as crop-milk for the first few days of life. One of the few birds that can drink without tilting its head back. Nests under bridges and on buildings, balconies, barns and sheds. Was once poisoned as a "nuisance city bird." Many cities now have Peregrine Falcons (not shown) that feed on Rock Pigeons, keeping their numbers in check.

Common urban Florida

breeding
pg. 165

displaying

winter

Willet
Catoptrophorus semipalmatus

Size: 15" (38 cm)

Male: Winter plumage is gray with a gray bill and legs. White belly. A distinctive black and white wing lining pattern, seen in flight or during display.

Female: same as male

Juvenile: similar to breeding adult, more tan in color

Nest: ground; female builds; 1 brood per year

Eggs: 3-5; olive green with dark markings

Incubation: 24-28 days; male and female incubate

Fledging: unknown days; female and male feed young

Migration: non-migrator to complete in coastal Florida

Food: aquatic insects

Compare: Very similar to the light gray winter Short-billed Dowitcher (pg. 245), which has a longer bill, yellow greenish legs and rarely looks up from its constant feeding. Lesser and Greater Yellowlegs (pp. 143 and 161, respectively) have yellow legs.

Stan's Notes: Common along coastal Florida during winter, with many continuing to migrate through the state to the coast of South America. Appears a rich, warm brown during breeding season and rather plain gray during winter, but always has a striking black and white wing pattern when seen in flight. Uses its black and white wing patches to display to its mate. Named for the "pill-will-willet" call it gives during the breeding season. Gives a "kip-kip-kip" alarm call when it takes flight. Nests on the East and Gulf coasts, in some western states and Canada.

Beaches Florida

female pg. 197

male

soaring

Northern Harrier
Circus cyaneus

WINTER

Size: 22-24" (56-60 cm); up to 3½-foot wingspan

Male: A slim, low-flying hawk. Silver gray with a large white rump patch and a white belly. Faint narrow bands across tail. Black wing tips. Yellow eyes.

Female: dark brown back, a brown-streaked breast and belly, large white rump patch, narrow black bands across the tail, black wing tips, yellow eyes

Juvenile: similar to female, with an orange breast

Nest: platform, often on ground; female and male build; 1 brood per year

Eggs: 4-8; bluish white without markings

Incubation: 31-32 days; female incubates

Fledging: 30-35 days; male and female feed young

Migration: complete, to Florida, other southern states, Mexico and Central America

Food: mice, snakes, insects, small birds

Compare: Slimmer than Red-tailed Hawk (pg. 187). Look for black tail bands, white rump patch and characteristic flight to help identify.

Stan's Notes: One of the easiest hawks to identify. Harriers glide just above ground, following contours of the land while searching for prey. Holds its wings just above the horizontal position, tilting back and forth in the wind, similar to Turkey Vultures. Formerly called Marsh Hawk due to its habit of hunting over marshes. Feeds on the ground. Will perch on the ground to preen and rest. At any age, has a distinctive owl-like face disk.

juvenile

YEAR-ROUND
SUMMER

Yellow-crowned Night-Heron
Nyctanassa violacea

Size: 24" (60 cm); up to 3½-foot wingspan

Male: Stocky gray heron with a black head, white crown and cheek patch. Dark thick bill and yellow legs. During breeding season, crown acquires a yellow hue.

Female: same as male

Juvenile: brown with white streaks and a dark bill, green legs

Nest: platform; female and male build; 1 brood per year

Eggs: 4-6; light blue without markings

Incubation: 21-25 days; female and male incubate

Fledging: 21-25 days; female and male feed young

Migration: non-migrator to partial in Florida

Food: aquatic insects, fish, crustaceans

Compare: One of many heron species in Florida. The distinctive patterned black and white head makes this heron easy to identify.

Stan's Notes: This heron hunts during the night, as the common name implies, but it can also be active during the day. Found in coastal mangroves to interior swamps, often hunting fiddler crabs and crayfish. Not uncommon for it to nest in large heron rookeries, and sometimes will nest by itself or in small colonies. Usually seen alone or in small groups. During the breeding season, the crown will acquire a yellow hue.

Ding Darling Reserve/ Sanibel

4- Safety Harbor Pier

in flight

Canada Goose
Branta canadensis

YEAR-ROUND

Size: 25-43" (63-109 cm); up to 5½-foot wingspan

Male: Large gray goose with a black neck and head and a white chin or cheek strap.

Female: same as male

Juvenile: same as adult

Nest: platform, on the ground; female builds; 1 brood per year

Eggs: 5-10; white without markings

Incubation: 25-30 days; female incubates

Fledging: 42-55 days; male and female teach young to feed

Migration: non-migrator in Florida

Food: aquatic plants, insects, seeds

Compare: Large goose that is rarely confused with any other bird.

Stan's Notes: A year-round resident in parts of northern Florida. Adults mate for many years, but only start to breed in their third year. Males often act as sentinels, standing at the edge of their group and bobbing their heads up and down, becoming very aggressive to anybody who approaches. Will hiss as if displaying displeasure. Adults molt primary flight feathers while raising young, rendering family groups flightless at the same time. Several subspecies vary geographically across the U.S. Generally they are paler in color in eastern groups and darker in western. Size decreases northward, with the smallest subspecies found on the Arctic tundra.

in flight

rusty stain

rusty stain in flight

Sandhill Crane
Grus canadensis

YEAR-ROUND
MIGRATION
WINTER

Size: 40-48" (102-120 cm); up to 7-foot wingspan

Male: Elegant gray bird with long legs and neck. Wings and body often stained rusty brown. Scarlet red cap. Yellow-to-red eyes.

Female: same as male

Juvenile: dull brown, lacks red cap, has yellow eyes

Nest: platform, on the ground; female and male build; 1 brood per year

Eggs: 2; olive with brown markings

Incubation: 28-32 days; female and male incubate

Fledging: 65 days; female and male feed young

Migration: complete to non-migrator in Florida

Food: insects, fruit, worms, plants, amphibians

Compare: Similar size as Great Blue Heron (pg. 265), but has a shorter bill and red cap. The Great Blue Heron flies with its neck held in an S shape unlike the straight neck of Sandhill Crane. The Tricolored Heron (pg. 95) has a blue head and wings and white undersides.

Stan's Notes: Among the tallest birds in the world and capable of flying at great heights. Usually seen in large undisturbed fields near water. Has a very distinctive rattling call. Often heard before seen. Plumage often appears rusty brown (see insets) due to staining from mud during preening. A characteristic flight with upstroke quicker than down. Performing a spectacular mating dance, the birds face each other, bow and jump into the air while uttering loud cackling sounds and flapping wings. Often flips sticks and grass into the air during dance.

I-4 Rest Station
Nov 24 - 2006

in flight

YEAR-ROUND

Great Blue Heron
Ardea herodias

Size: 42-52" (107-132 cm); up to 6-foot wingspan

Male: Tall gray heron. Black eyebrows extend into several long plumes off the back of head. Long yellow bill. Feathers at base of neck drop down in a kind of necklace.

Female: same as male

Juvenile: same as adult, but more brown than gray, with a black crown and no plumes

Nest: platform; male and female build; 1 brood per year

Eggs: 3-5; blue green without markings

Incubation: 27-28 days; female and male incubate

Fledging: 56-60 days; male and female feed young

Migration: non-migrator in Florida

Food: small fish, frogs, insects, snakes

Compare: Similar size as the Sandhill Crane (pg. 263), but lacks a red crown. The Sandhill Crane flies with its neck held straight unlike the Heron's S shaped neck. Tricolored Heron (pg. 95) is half the size of the Great Blue Heron and has a white belly.

Stan's Notes: One of the most common herons, often barking like a dog when startled. Seen stalking small fish in shallow water. Will strike at mice, squirrels and just about anything else it might come across. Flies holding neck in an S shape, with its long legs trailing straight out behind. The wings are held in cupped fashion during flight. Nests in colonies of up to 100 birds. Nests in treetops near or over open water.

common Beaches   Old Tampa Bay   Low tide

SUMMER
WINTER

Ruby-throated Hummingbird
Archilochus colubris

Size: 3-3½" (7.5-9 cm)

Male: Tiny iridescent green bird with black throat patch that reflects bright ruby red in sun.

Female: same as male, but lacking the throat patch

Juvenile: same as female

Nest: cup; female builds; 1-2 broods per year

Eggs: 2; white without markings

Incubation: 12-14 days; female incubates

Fledging: 14-18 days; female feeds young

Migration: complete, to southern Florida, other southern states, Mexico and Central America

Food: nectar, insects; will come to nectar feeders

Compare: No other bird is as tiny. The Sphinx Moth also hovers at flowers, but has clear wings and a mouth part that looks like a straw, which coils up when not at flowers. Doesn't hum in flight, moves much slower than the Hummingbird and can be approached.

Stan's Notes: The smallest bird in the state. Can hover, fly up and down, and is the only bird to fly backward. Does not sing, but will chatter or buzz to communicate. The wings create a humming noise, flapping 50-60 times each second or faster during chasing flights. The heart pumps an incredible 1,260 beats per minute, and it breathes 250 times per minute. Weighing just 2-3 grams, it takes about five average-sized hummingbirds to equal the weight of one chickadee. Constructs its nest with plant material and spider webs, gluing pieces of lichen on the outside for camouflage. Attracted to tubular red flowers.

 CD 2, TRACK 54

male

female

Painted Bunting
Passerina ciris

Size: 5½" (14 cm)

Male: An amazing combination of colors. A green back, deep blue head and orange chest and belly. Dark wings and tail.

Female: bright green above, light green below

Juvenile: drab version of the female with only some small spots of green

Nest: cup; female and male construct; 1-2 broods per year

Eggs: 3-5; pale blue with brown markings

Incubation: 11-12 days; female incubate

Fledging: 12-14 days; female and male feed young

Migration: complete, to Florida, other southern states, Bahamas, Cuba, Mexico, Central America

Food: seeds, insects; will visit seed feeders

Compare: No other bird can compare with the male's striking colors. The female is uniquely green and rarely confused with any other bird.

Stan's Notes: A wonderful bunting of backyard gardens, woodland edges and along brushy roads. Visits seed feeders in wooded yards. Well known for its loud, clear and varied warbling phrases. Cup nest, made of grass and lined with animal hair, is usually in a deep, tangled mass of vines. A common cowbird host, this unfortunately often results in raising the cowbird young only and not its own. Although it winters in the southern half of Florida, most continue to migrate southward. More well known in Oklahoma and Texas. Often captured in Central America and sold as a caged bird; both activities are illegal in the U.S. and should not be supported.

MIGRATION
SUMMER
WINTER

Monk Parakeet

Myiopsitta monachus

YEAR-ROUND

Size: 12" (30 cm)

Male: A lime green back and belly. Gray forehead extending into chest. Tips and trailing edge of wings are blue. A short, hooked yellow bill. Long narrow tail.

Female: same as male

Juvenile: same as adult

Nest: cavity, in a large stick nest; female and male build; 1 brood per year

Eggs: 4-6; off-white without markings

Incubation: 12-14 days; female incubates

Fledging: 28-30 days; female and male feed young

Migration: non-migrator

Food: fruit, seeds

Compare: Several parakeet species occur in Florida, but the Monk Parakeet is the most widespread in southern Florida. Usually seen in urban parks.

Stan's Notes: The Monk Parakeet has two toes pointing forward and two toes back. This is unlike other birds, which have three toes pointing forward and one back. The toe arrangement helps the foot hold food while bringing it to the mouth. Builds a huge colony nest from sticks. There are over 300 parakeet species in the world. The Monk Parakeet, which breeds in southern Florida, is originally from Argentina. The only native North American parakeet was the Carolina Parakeet. Now extinct, it was last reported in Florida in the 1920s. All parakeets currently in Florida came from release or are escaped pets.

plenty - common urban

 CD 2, TRACK 56

271

female pg. 181

male

Wood Duck
Aix sponsa

YEAR-ROUND
WINTER

Size: 17-20" (43-50 cm)

Male: A small, highly ornamented dabbling duck with a green head and crest patterned with white and black. A rusty chest, white belly and red eyes.

Female: brown, similar size and shape as male, has bright white eye-ring and a not-so-obvious crest, blue patch on wing often hidden

Juvenile: same as female

Nest: cavity; female lines old woodpecker cavity; 1 brood per year

Eggs: 10-15; creamy white without markings

Incubation: 28-36 days; female incubates

Fledging: 56-68 days; female teaches young to feed

Migration: non-migrator to partial in Florida

Food: aquatic insects, plants, seeds

Compare: Smaller than the male Northern Shoveler (pg. 277) and lacks the long wide bill.

Stan's Notes: A common duck of quiet, shallow backwater ponds. Nearly extinct around 1900 due to overhunting, but is doing well now. Nests in an old woodpecker hole or uses a nesting box. Often seen flying deep in forests or perched high on tree branches. Female takes to flight with a loud squealing call and enters nest cavity from full flight. Lays eggs in a neighboring female nest (egg dumping), resulting in some clutches in excess of 20 eggs. Young stay in nest 24 hours after hatching, then jump from up to 30 feet (9 m) to the ground or water to follow their mother, never returning to the nest.

plenty - common
urban

Green Heron
Butorides virescens

YEAR-ROUND
SUMMER

Size: 16-22" (40-56 cm)

Male: Short stocky heron with a blue-green back, and rusty red neck and chest. Dark green crest. Short legs, normally yellow, but turn bright orange during breeding season.

Female: same as male

Juvenile: similar to adult, with a blue-gray back and white-streaked chest and neck

Nest: platform; female and male build; 2 broods per year

Eggs: 2-4; light green without markings

Incubation: 21-25 days; female and male incubate

Fledging: 35-36 days; female and male feed young

Migration: non-migrator to complete in Florida

Food: fish, insects, amphibians, aquatic plants

Compare: Green Heron is smaller than the Tricolored Heron (pg. 95) and lacks the long neck of most other herons. Also much smaller than the Great Blue Heron (pg. 265). Look for a small heron with a dark green back and crest stalking wetlands.

Stan's Notes: Often gives an explosive, rasping "skyew" call when startled. Sometimes it looks like it doesn't have a neck, because it holds its head close to its body. Hunts for small fish, aquatic insects and small amphibians by waiting on a shore or wading stealthily. Known to place an object such as an insect on the water surface to attract fish to catch. Raises its crest when excited.

CD 2, TRACK 57

275

female pg. 183

male

Northern Shoveler
Anas clypeata

Size: 20" (50 cm)

Male: Medium-sized duck with iridescent green head, rusty sides and white breast. Has an extraordinarily large spoon-shaped bill that is almost always held pointed toward water.

Female: brown and black all over, blue wing patch, spoon-shaped bill

Juvenile: same as female

Nest: ground; female builds; 1 brood per year

Eggs: 9-12; olive without markings

Incubation: 22-25 days; female incubates

Fledging: 30-60 days; female leads young to food

Migration: complete, to Florida, other southern states, Mexico and Central America

Food: aquatic insects, plants

Compare: Similar to the male Mallard (pg. 281), but Shoveler has a large, characteristic spoon-shaped bill. Larger than male Wood Duck (pg. 273) and lacks the Wood Duck's crest.

Stan's Notes: One of several species of shoveler, so called because of the peculiar shape of its bill. The Northern Shoveler is the only species of these ducks in North America. Found in small flocks of 5-10, swimming low in water with its large bill pointed toward the water, as if it's too heavy to lift. Feeds mainly by filtering tiny aquatic insects and plants from the water's surface with its bill. This winter visitor arrives in Florida in September and leaves in April.

female pg. 195

male

MIGRATION
WINTER

Red-breasted Merganser
Mergus serrator

Size: 23" (58 cm)

Male: A shaggy green head and crest. Prominent white collar. Rusty breast. Black and white body. Long orange bill.

Female: overall brown to gray with a shaggy reddish head and crest, long orange bill

Juvenile: similar to female

Nest: ground; female builds; 1 brood per year

Eggs: 5-10; olive green without markings

Incubation: 29-30 days; female incubates

Fledging: 55-65 days; female feeds young

Migration: complete, to coastal Florida

Food: fish, aquatic insects

Compare: The male Hooded Merganser (pg. 55) has a large white patch on the head unlike the green head of male Red-breasted Merganser.

Stan's Notes: A winter resident in coastal Florida. This is the most common of the wintering mergansers, arriving in late October and leaving in April. Most commonly seen along the Florida coast, but can also be seen in large inland freshwater lakes. A very fast flier, clocked at up to 100 miles (161 km) per hour. Often seen flying low across the water. Needs a long run for takeoff with wings flapping to get airborne. Serrated bill helps it catch slippery fish. Usually is a silent duck. Male sometimes gives a soft, catlike meow. Female gives a harsh "krrr-croak." Doesn't breed before 2 years of age. The male will abandon the female just after eggs are laid. Females often share nests. Breeds across Alaska and northern Canada. The young leave the nest within 24 hours of hatching, never to return.

female pg. 199

male

YEAR-ROUND

Mallard
Anas platyrhynchos

Size: 27-28" (69-71 cm)

Male: Large, bulbous green head, white necklace and rust brown or chestnut chest. Gray and white on the sides. Yellow bill. Orange legs and feet.

Female: brown duck with an orange and black bill and blue and white wing mark (speculum)

Juvenile: same as female, but with a yellow bill

Nest: ground; female builds; 1 brood per year

Eggs: 7-10; greenish to whitish, unmarked

Incubation: 26-30 days; female incubates

Fledging: 42-52 days; female leads young to food

Migration: non-migrator in Florida

Food: seeds, plants, aquatic insects; will come to ground feeders offering corn

Compare: Most people recognize this common duck. Male Red-breasted Merganser (pg. 279) has a shaggy crest and an orange bill. The male Northern Shoveler (pg. 277) has a white breast with rust on the sides and a large spoon-shaped bill.

Stan's Notes: A familiar duck of lakes and ponds, it's considered a type of dabbling duck, tipping forward in shallow water to feed on aquatic plants on the bottom. The name "Mallard" comes from the Latin *masculus*, meaning "male," referring to the habit of males not taking part in raising ducklings. Black central tail feathers of male curl upward. Both the male and female have white tails and white underwings. Will return to place of birth.

common on ponds

female pg. 321

male

American Redstart
Setophaga ruticilla

MIGRATION
WINTER

Size: 5" (13 cm)

Male: Small, striking black bird with contrasting patches of orange on sides, wings and tail. White belly

Female: olive brown with yellow patches on sides, wings and tail, white belly

Juvenile: same as female, the juvenile male is tinged orange in the first year

Nest: cup; female builds; 1 brood per year

Eggs: 3-5; off-white with brown markings

Incubation: 12 days; female incubates

Fledging: 9 days; female and male feed young

Migration: complete, to southern Florida, Mexico and Central and South America

Food: insects, seeds, berries rarely

Compare: Male Red-winged Blackbird (pg. 9) and the male Baltimore Oriole (pg. 285) are much larger at roughly 8 inches (20 cm). The only small black and orange bird flitting around the tops of trees.

Stan's Notes: A common, widespread warbler in the state during migration and winter. Prefers large unbroken tracts of forest. This bird appears to be hyperactive when feeding, hovering and darting back and forth to glean insects from leaves. Often droops its wings and fans tail just before launching out to catch an insect. Look for the male's flashing black and orange colors high up in trees.

CD 2, TRACK 58

male

female pg. 329

Baltimore Oriole
Icterus galbula

MIGRATION
WINTER

Size: 7-8" (18-20 cm)

Male: Bright flaming orange bird with black head and black extending down nape of neck onto the back. Black wings with white and orange wing bars. An orange tail with black streaks. Gray bill and dark eyes.

Female: pale yellow with orange tones, gray brown wings, white wing bars, gray bill, dark eyes

Juvenile: same as female

Nest: pendulous; female builds; 1 brood per year

Eggs: 4-5; bluish with brown markings

Incubation: 12-14 days; female incubates

Fledging: 12-14 days; female and male feed young

Migration: complete, to Florida, Mexico, Central and South America

Food: insects, fruit, nectar; comes to orange half and nectar feeders

Compare: Male Orchard Oriole (pg. 287) is a much darker orange than the flaming orange of the male Baltimore Oriole. Male American Redstart (pg. 283) is smaller and has more black than orange.

Stan's Notes: A fantastic songster, this bird is often heard before seen. Easily attracted to a feeder offering grape jelly, orange halves or sugar water (nectar). Parents bring young to feeders. Sits in tops of trees feeding on caterpillars. Female builds a sock-like nest at the outermost branches of tall trees. Often returns to the same area year after year. Usually seen during migration and winter.

 CD 2, TRACK 59

female pg. 331

male

Orchard Oriole
Icterus spurius

SUMMER

Size: 7-8" (18-20 cm)

Male: Dull orange oriole with a black head, chin, wings and tail, and black extending down the back. Single white wing bars. Long, thin black bill with a small gray mark on lower mandible (jaw).

Female: olive green back with a dull yellow belly, 2 white wing bars on dark gray wings

Juvenile: same as female, black bib on first-year male

Nest: pendulous; female builds; 1 brood per year

Eggs: 3-5; pale blue to white, brown markings

Incubation: 11-12 days; female and male incubate

Fledging: 11-14 days; female and male feed young

Migration: complete, to Mexico, Central America and northern South America

Food: insects, fruit; comes to fruit/nectar feeders

Compare: Similar to male Baltimore Oriole (pg. 285), but the male Orchard Oriole has a much darker orange body.

Stan's Notes: Prefers orchards or open woods, hence its common name. Eats insects until wild fruit starts to ripen. Summer resident in the northern part of Florida. Often nests alone, but sometimes nests in small colonies. Parents bring young to jelly and orange half feeders just after fledging. Many think the orioles have left during the summer, but the birds are concentrating on finding insects to feed their young.

male

female pg. 101

yellow male

House Finch
Carpodacus mexicanus

YEAR-ROUND

Size: 5" (13 cm)

Male: An orange red face, breast and rump, with a brown cap. Brown marking behind eyes. Brown wings streaked with white. A white belly with brown streaks.

Female: brown with a heavily streaked white chest

Juvenile: similar to female

Nest: cup, sometimes in cavities; female builds; 2 broods per year

Eggs: 4-5; pale blue, lightly marked

Incubation: 12-14 days; female incubates

Fledging: 15-19 days; female and male feed young

Migration: non-migrator to partial; will move around to find food

Food: seeds, fruit, leaf buds; will visit seed feeders

Compare: Male Purple Finch (pg. 291) is very similar, but male House Finch lacks the red crown. Look for the streaked breast and belly, and brown cap of male House Finch.

Stan's Notes: Very social bird. Visits feeders in small flocks. Likes nesting in hanging flower baskets. Incubating female is fed by the male. Has a loud, cheerful warbling song. House Finches that were originally introduced to Long Island, New York, from the western U.S. in the 1940s have since populated the entire eastern U.S. Now found throughout the country. Can be the most common bird at your feeders. Suffers from a fatal eye disease that causes the eyes to crust over. Rarely, some males are yellow (see inset) instead of red, probably due to poor diet.

CD 1, TRACK 49

female
pg. 111

male

WINTER

Purple Finch
Carpodacus purpureus

Size: 6" (15 cm)

Male: Raspberry red head, cap, breast, back and rump. Brownish wings and tail.

Female: heavily streaked brown and white bird with large white eyebrows

Juvenile: same as female

Nest: cup; female and male construct; 1 brood per year

Eggs: 4-5; greenish blue with brown markings

Incubation: 12-13 days; female incubates

Fledging: 13-14 days; female and male feed young

Migration: irruptive; moves around in winter in search of food

Food: seeds, insects, fruit; comes to seed feeders

Compare: Redder than the orange red of male House Finch (pg. 289), with a clear breast. Male House Finch has a brown cap unlike male Purple Finch's red cap.

Stan's Notes: Usually seen only during winter in northern Florida, when flocks of Purple Finches leave their homes farther north and move around searching for food. Will visit seed feeders along with House Finches, making it difficult to tell them apart. Feeds mainly on seeds. Prefers open woods or woodland edges. Travels in flocks of up to 50. Has a rich loud song, with a distinctive "tic" note made only in flight. Not a purple color, the Latin species name *purpureus* means "crimson" or other reddish color.

 CD 1, TRACK 53

female
pg. 333

male

Summer Tanager
Piranga rubra

YEAR-ROUND
SUMMER
WINTER

Size: 8" (20 cm)

Male: Bright rosy red bird with darker red wings.

Female: overall yellow with slightly darker wings

Juvenile: male has patches of red and green over the entire body, female is same as adult female

Nest: cup; female builds; 1-2 broods per year

Eggs: 3-5; pale blue with dark markings

Incubation: 10-12 days; female incubates

Fledging: unknown days; female and male feed young

Migration: complete, to Florida, Central America and South America

Food: insects, fruit

Compare: Similar size as the male Northern Cardinal (pg. 295), but the male Cardinal has a black mask, large crest and red bill.

Stan's Notes: A distinctive bird of woodlands in Florida, especially in mixed pine and oak forests. Due to the clearing of land for agriculture, populations have decreased over the past 100 years and especially in the last 20 years. Returning to Florida in late March and with young hatching in May, some pairs have two broods per year. Most leave the state by November with very few remaining for winter. While fruit makes up some of the diet, most of it consists of insects such as bees and wasps. Summer Tanagers unfortunately seem to be parasitized by Brown-headed Cowbirds more than just about any other nesting bird in Florida.

 CD 2, TRACK 61

female pg. 133

male

juvenile

YEAR-ROUND

Northern Cardinal
Cardinalis cardinalis

Size: 8-9" (20-22.5 cm)

Male: All-red bird with a black mask that extends from the face down to the chin and throat. Large red bill and crest.

Female: buff brown with tinges of red on crest and wings, same black mask and red bill

Juvenile: same as female, but with a blackish gray bill

Nest: cup; female builds; 2-3 broods per year

Eggs: 3-4; bluish white with brown markings

Incubation: 12-13 days; female and male incubate

Fledging: 9-10 days; female and male feed young

Migration: non-migrator

Food: seeds, insects, fruit; comes to seed feeders

Compare: Similar size as the male Summer Tanager (pg. 293), but the male Tanager is rosy red. Look for Northern Cardinal's black mask, large crest and red bill.

Stan's Notes: A familiar backyard bird. Look for the male feeding female during courtship. Male feeds young of the first brood by himself while female builds second nest. The name comes from the Latin word *cardinalis*, which means "important." Very territorial in spring, it will fight its own reflection in a window. Non-territorial during winter, gathering in small flocks of up to 20 birds. Both the male and female sing and can be heard anytime of year. Listen for its "whata-cheer-cheer-cheer" territorial call in the spring.

in flight

juvenile

Roseate Spoonbill
Platalea ajaja

Size: 32" (80 cm); up to 4-foot wingspan

Male: An overall pink bird with red highlights. A white neck with a black patch on the back of the head. A heavy, spoon-shaped flat bill. Long red legs.

Female: same as male

Juvenile: pale version of adult

Nest: platform; female and male build; 1 brood per year

Eggs: 1-4; olive green with dark markings

Incubation: 22-23 days; male and female incubate

Fledging: 35-42 days; female and male feed young

Migration: partial to non-migrator

Food: fish, aquatic insects, snails, worms, leeches

Compare: This is an unmistakable bird of Florida. The Roseate Spoonbill is larger than White Ibis (pg. 315), which has a long, down-curved orange-to-red bill unlike the heavy flat bill of the Spoonbill.

Stan's Notes: A coastal resident of Florida. This bird is making a comeback from devastating hunting pressures in the 1800s for its wing feathers, which were used in women's hats and fans. Now habitat destruction is limiting its numbers. Swings its spoon-shaped bill to sift fish and insects from shallow waters. Usually seen in small flocks. Nests in mixed colonies with herons. Related to the ibises.

Old Tampa Bay
Phillipe Park
Ding Darling Reserve
Sanibel

in flight

Least Tern
Sterna antillarum

SUMMER

Size: 9" (22.5 cm)

Male: A white and gray tern with a black cap and white forehead. Bill is light orange-yellow with a dark tip. White belly. Leg color is the same as the bill. Black wing tips and a short, deeply forked tail, seen in flight.

Female: same as male

Juvenile: browner version of adult, with a dark bill and partial black cap during first summer

Nest: ground; female builds; 1 brood per year

Eggs: 1-3; olive green with dark markings

Incubation: 20-22 days; female incubates

Fledging: 19-20 days; female teaches young to feed

Migration: complete, to South America

Food: aquatic insects, fish

Compare: Half the size of Royal Tern (pg. 307), which has black legs and a large orange-red bill unlike the Least Tern's smaller, dark-tipped orange-yellow bill. In flight, look for black wing tips and a short, deeply forked tail.

Stan's Notes: The smallest tern in North America, the Least Tern is also an endangered species in many North American locations. Killed by the hundreds of thousands in the early 1900s for its feathers. Its decreasing numbers are now due to predators such as cats and dogs and human disturbance while nesting. Nests in large colonies on sandy beaches. Will often hover over intruders in the colony. Hunts small fish and aquatic insects by plunging into water or skimming over the surface. Recognizes mate by distinctive calls.

 CD 2, TRACK 63

in flight

Forster's Tern
Sterna forsteri

WINTER

Size: 14-15" (36-38 cm)

Male: White and gray tern with a jet black crown and an orange bill with a black tip. Leading edge of wings is gray, trailing edge is white. Characteristic forked tail is long and white. Winter plumage lacks the black crown and the bill becomes nearly entirely black.

Female: same as male

Juvenile: similar to adult, lacks the black crown

Nest: floating platform; female and male build; 1 brood per year

Eggs: 3-5; tan to white with brown markings

Incubation: 23-24 days; female and male incubate

Fledging: 24-26 days; male and female feed young

Migration: complete, to Florida, other southern coastal states, Mexico and Central America

Food: small fish, aquatic insects

Compare: Smaller than Royal Tern (pg. 307), which has a larger orange-red bill. Look for a jet black crown, orange bill with black tip and white tips of wings. Least Tern (pg. 299) is smaller and has a lighter orange-yellow bill.

Stan's Notes: Usually seen in small colonies. Catches small fish by diving into the water headfirst. Will catch insects in flight. Builds a platform nest on floating vegetation. Nests in small colonies in shallow water marshes. Was named after Johann Reinhold Forster, a German naturalist who traveled around the world with Captain Cook in 1772.

 CD 2, TRACK 64

in flight

breeding

in flight

winter

Laughing Gull
Larus atricilla

YEAR-ROUND
WINTER

Size: 16-17" (40-43 cm); up to 3⅓-foot wingspan

Male: Breeding adult has a black head "hood" and white neck, chest and belly. Slate gray back and wings with black wing tips. Orange bill. Incomplete white eye-ring. Winter plumage lacks the "hood" and has a black bill.

Female: same as male

Juvenile: brown throughout, gray sides, lacking the black head and white chest, has a gray bill

Nest: ground; male and female construct; 1 brood per year

Eggs: 2-4; olive with brown markings

Incubation: 18-20 days; female and male incubate

Fledging: 30-35 days; male and female feed young

Migration: non-migrator to partial in Florida

Food: fish, insects, aquatic insects

Compare: Smaller than the Ring-billed Gull (pg. 305) and Herring Gull (pg. 313). Look for the black head "hood" and slate gray back and wings of the Laughing Gull.

Stan's Notes: This is a three-year gull that starts out mostly brown and gray. The second year it resembles adults, but lacks a complete black head "hood." Breeding plumage in the third year. Male tosses its head back and calls to attract a mate. Nests in marshes in large colonies. Nest is a scrape on the ground lined with grass, sticks and rocks. Adults regurgitate food to feed young.

Very Common on Beaches

in flight

breeding

juvenile

winter

WINTER

Ring-billed Gull
Larus delawarensis

Size: 19" (48 cm); up to 4-foot wingspan

Male: A white bird with gray wings, black wing tips spotted with white, and a white tail, as seen in flight. Yellow bill with a black ring near tip. Yellowish legs and feet. Winter or non-breeding adult has a speckled brown back of head and nape of neck.

Female: same as male

Juvenile: mostly gray version of winter adult, has a dark band at end of tail

Nest: ground; female and male construct; 1 brood per year

Eggs: 2-4; off-white with brown markings

Incubation: 20-21 days; female and male incubate

Fledging: 20-40 days; female and male feed young

Migration: complete, to Florida, other southern states and Mexico

Food: insects, fish; scavenges for food

Compare: Laughing Gull (pg. 303) has a black head "hood." The Herring Gull (pg. 313) has an orange-red mark on its lower bill, pink legs and lacks Ring-billed's black ring on bill.

Stan's Notes: A common gull of garbage dumps and parking lots. This bird is expanding its range and remaining farther north longer during winter due to successful scavenging in cities. A three-year gull with different plumages in its first three autumns. Attains the ring on bill after its first winter and adult plumage in the third year. Defends a small area around nest.

CD 2, TRACK 66 *Beaches*

winter

in flight

breeding

Royal Tern
Sterna maxima

YEAR-ROUND
WINTER

Size: 20" (50 cm)

Male: Gray back and upper surface of wings with white below. Large orange-red bill. Forked tail. Black legs and feet. Breeding plumage has a black cap extending down the nape. Winter plumage has a white forehead and only a partial black cap.

Female: same as male

Juvenile: dull white to gray with only a hint of a black cap that rarely extends down the nape

Nest: ground; female and male build; 1-2 broods per year

Eggs: 1-2; off-white with dark brown markings

Incubation: 30-31 days; female and male incubate

Fledging: 28-35 days; female and male feed young

Migration: complete to non-migrator, to coastal Florida

Food: fish, aquatic insects

Compare: Larger than Forster's Tern (pg. 301), which has a small black-tipped bill. Twice the size of Least Tern (pg. 299), which has a lighter orange-yellow bill and a shorter forked tail.

Stan's Notes: Winter resident along coastal Florida. Nests in large colonies on islands in the Banana River and Tampa Bay, and other places in southern coastal Florida. Lays one egg (rarely two) in a shallow depression on the ground. Like other terns, Royal Terns plunge from heights 40 feet (12 m) and more into water headfirst to capture fish and aquatic insects.

Common
Fort de Soto Park

CD 2, TRACK 67

Cattle Egret
Bubulcus ibis

Size: 20" (50 cm); up to 3-foot wingspan

Male: Stocky with a disproportional large round head. White with orange buff crest, breast and back. Red-orange bill and legs. Winter plumage is all white with a yellow bill and dark legs.

Female: same as male

Juvenile: similar to winter adult, with a dark bill

Nest: platform; female and male build; 1 brood per year

Eggs: 2-5; light blue green without markings

Incubation: 22-26 days; female and male incubate

Fledging: 28-30 days; female and male feed young

Migration: partial to non-migrator in Florida; moves around to find food

Food: insects, small mammals

Compare: About half the size of Great Egret (pg. 317), which has a much longer neck and a much larger bill. White Ibis (pg. 315) has a large down-curved bill.

Stan's Notes: Came to South America from Africa around 1880, reaching Florida in the 1940s. Often seen singularly in pastures, hunting insects at cow and horse pies. Holding its head still while wiggling its neck back and forth and from side to side, it stabs at prey, captures it, then tosses it to the back of its mouth in one swift move. Frequently attracted to field fires to hunt newly exposed insects and animals. In some years it is found as far as northern tier states and Canada. *I 75 N along Ditches in small Flocks*

in flight

YEAR-ROUND
SUMMER

Snowy Egret
Egretta thula

Size: 24" (60 cm); up to 3½-foot wingspan

Male: All-white bird. Black bill. Black legs. Bright yellow feet. Long feather plumes on head, neck and back during breeding season.

Female: same as male

Juvenile: similar to adult, but backs of legs are yellow

Nest: platform; female and male build; 1 brood per year

Eggs: 3-5; light blue-green without markings

Incubation: 20-24 days; female and male incubate

Fledging: 28-30 days; female and male feed young

Migration: non-migrator to complete in Florida

Food: aquatic insects, small fish

Compare: Much smaller than Great Egret (pg. 317), which has a yellow bill and black feet. Look for the black bill and yellow feet of Snowy Egret to help identify. Same size as juvenile Little Blue Heron (pg. 93), which has a black-tipped gray bill.

Stan's Notes: Common in wetlands and often seen with other egrets. Colonies may include up to several hundred nests. Nests are low in shrubs 5-10 feet (1.5-3 m) tall or are on the ground, usually mixed among other egret and heron nests. Chicks hatch days apart (asynchronous), leading to starvation of last to hatch. Will actively "hunt" prey by moving around quickly, stirring up small fish and aquatic insects with its feet. In the breeding state, a yellow patch at the base of bill and the yellow feet turn orange-red. Was hunted to near extinction in the late 1800s for its feathers,

breeding

winter

juvenile

Herring Gull
Larus argentatus

WINTER

Size: 23-26" (58-66 cm); up to 5-foot wingspan

Male: Snow-white bird with slate gray wings and black wing tips with tiny white spots. Bill is yellow with an orange-red spot near the tip of lower bill. Pinkish legs. Winter plumage head and neck are dirty gray to brown.

Female: same as male

Juvenile: uniformly mottled brown to gray, black bill

Nest: ground; female and male construct; 1 brood per year

Eggs: 2-3; olive with brown markings

Incubation: 24-28 days; female and male incubate

Fledging: 35-36 days; female and male feed young

Migration: complete, to coastal Florida, other southern coastal states

Food: fish, insects, clams, eggs, baby birds

Compare: Larger than the King-billed Gull (pg. 305), which has yellowish legs, a black ring near the tip of its bill and lacks the orange-red spot on its lower mandible.

Stan's Notes: Common gull of large lakes. An opportunistic bird, scavenging for food from dumpsters, but will also take other birds' eggs and young right from nest. Often drops clams and other shell-fish from heights to break shells and get to the soft interior. Nests in colonies, returning to same site year after year. Lines ground nest with grasses and seaweed. Takes about four years for juveniles to obtain adult plumage. Adults molt to a dirty gray in the winter, and look similar to juveniles.

Common Sanibel Island

 CD 2, TRACK 70

juvenile

YEAR-ROUND
SUMMER

White Ibis
Eudocimus albus

Size: 25" (63 cm); up to 3-foot wingspan

Male: All-white bird with a very long, downward curving orange-to-red bill. Pink facial skin. Color of legs matches the bill color. Black wing tips, seen only in flight.

Female: same as male, but smaller, downward curve of bill is less than curve of male bill

Juvenile: combination of chocolate brown and white for the first two years, dull orange bill

Nest: platform; female and male build; 1 brood per year

Eggs: 2-3; light blue with dark markings

Incubation: 21-23 days; female and male incubate

Fledging: 28-35 days; female and male feed young

Migration: non-migrator to partial in Florida

Food: aquatic insects, crustaceans, fish

Compare: White Ibis is completely white unlike the brown Glossy Ibis (pg. 193). Snowy Egret (pg. 309) has a straight black bill and bright yellow feet. Winter Cattle Egret (pg. 309) has a short yellow bill. Wood Stork (pg. 71) has a bald dark head and thick bill.

Stan's Notes: More common in southern Florida. It prefers fresh water over salt water, with crayfish a big part of its diet. The white plumage, black wing tips and bright bill make it easy to identify. Often flies in groups of 30 or more. Nests in large colonies in well-made stick nests. Hybridizes with the non-native all-red Scarlet Ibis (not shown) and produces young in various shades of pink or red.

common   Safety Harbor

 CD 2, TRACK 71

in flight

Great Egret
Ardea alba

Size: 38" (96 cm); up to 4½-foot wingspan

Male: Tall, thin, elegant all-white bird with a long, pointed yellow bill. Black stilt-like legs and black feet.

Female: same as male

Juvenile: same as adult

Nest: platform; male and female build; 1 brood per year

Eggs: 2-3; light blue without markings

Incubation: 23-26 days; female and male incubate

Fledging: 43-49 days; female and male feed young

Migration: non-migrator to partial in Florida

Food: fish, aquatic insects, frogs, crayfish

Compare: Cattle Egret (pg. 317) is about half the size of Great Egret and has a much shorter neck and much smaller bill. The Snowy Egret (pg. 311) is much smaller with yellow feet and a black bill. Larger than juvenile Little Blue Heron (pg. 93), which has a black-tipped gray bill. White Ibis (pg. 315) has a very long, down-curved orange-to-red bill.

Stan's Notes: A tall and stately bird, the Great Egret slowly stalks shallow wetlands looking for small fish to spear with its long sharp bill. Nests in colonies of up to 100 individuals. Now protected, it was hunted to near extinction in the 1800s and early 1900s for its long white plumage. The common name "Egret" came from the French word *aigrette*, which means "ornamental tufts of plumes." The plumes grow near the tail during breeding season.

breeding

in flight

chick-feeding
adult

MIGRATION
WINTER

American White Pelican
Pelecanus erythrorhynchos

Size: 62" (158 cm); up to 9-foot wingspan

Male: A large white bird with black wing tips that extend partially down the trailing edge of wings. A white or pale yellow crown. Bright yellow bill, legs and feet. Breeding adult has a bright orange bill and legs. An adult that is feeding chicks (chick-feeding adult) has a gray-black crown.

Female: same as male

Juvenile: duller white with brownish head and neck

Nest: ground, a scraped-out depression rimmed with dirt; female and male build; 1 brood per year

Eggs: 1-3; white without markings

Incubation: 29-36 days; male and female incubate

Fledging: 60-70 days; female and male feed young

Migration: complete, to Florida and Mexico

Food: fish

Compare: Very similar to the Brown Pelican (pg. 203), but is white with a bright yellow or orange bill. Look for black wing tips in flight.

Stan's Notes: Often seen in large groups on larger lakes. They feed by simultaneously dipping their bills in water to scoop up fish. They don't dive in water to catch fish, like coastal Brown Pelicans. Bills and legs of breeding adults turn deep orange. Breeding adults usually also grow a flat fibrous plate in the middle of the upper mandible. This plate drops off after eggs have hatched. They fly in a large V, often gliding with long wings, then all flapping together.

 CD 2, TRACK 73

Ding Darling - Sanibel
Ringling House - Sarasoto

male pg. 283

female

American Redstart
Setophaga ruticilla

MIGRATION
WINTER

Size: 5" (13 cm)

Female: Olive brown with yellow patches on sides, wings and tail. White belly.

Male: small, striking black bird with contrasting patches of orange on sides, wings and tail, white belly

Juvenile: same as female, the juvenile male is tinged orange in the first year

Nest: cup; female builds; 1 brood per year

Eggs: 3-5; off-white with brown markings

Incubation: 12 days; female incubates

Fledging: 9 days; female and male feed young

Migration: complete, to southern Florida, Mexico and Central and South America

Food: insects, seeds, berries rarely

Compare: Similar to female Yellow-rumped Warbler (pg. 211), but lacks the Yellow-rumped's yellow patch on rump.

Stan's Notes: A common, widespread warbler in the state during migration and winter. Prefers large unbroken tracts of forest. This bird appears to be hyperactive when feeding, hovering and darting back and forth to glean insects from leaves. Often droops its wings and fans tail just before launching out to catch an insect. Look for the male's flashing black and orange colors high up in trees.

winter male

male

female

WINTER

American Goldfinch
Carduelis tristis

Size: 5" (13 cm)

Male: A perky yellow bird with a black patch on forehead. Black tail with conspicuous white rump. Black wings with white wing bars. No marking on the chest. Dramatic change in color during winter, similar to female.

Female: dull olive yellow without a black forehead, with brown wings and a white rump

Juvenile: same as female

Nest: cup; female builds; 1 brood per year

Eggs: 4-6; pale blue without markings

Incubation: 10-12 days; female incubates

Fledging: 11-17 days; female and male feed young

Migration: partial migrator; flocks of up to 20 individuals move around North America

Food: seeds, insects; will come to seed feeders

Compare: The female House Finch (pg. 101) has a heavily streaked breast. The female Purple Finch (pg. 111) has white eyebrows and a heavily streaked breast.

Stan's Notes: Most often found in open fields, scrubby areas and woodlands. Often called Wild Canary. A feeder bird that enjoys Nyjer thistle. Late summer nesting, uses the silky down from wild thistle for nest. Appears roller-coaster-like in flight. Listen for it to twitter during flight. Almost always seen in small flocks. Moves into Florida for the winter starting in November. Can be a common visitor to feeders all winter, leaving in April for northern states.

 CD 2, TRACK 74

Common Yellowthroat
Geothlypis trichas

Size: 5" (13 cm)

Male: Olive brown bird with bright yellow throat and breast, a white belly and a distinctive black mask outlined in white. A long, thin, pointed black bill.

Female: similar to male, lacks the black mask

Juvenile: same as female

Nest: cup; female builds; 2 broods per year

Eggs: 3-5; white with brown markings

Incubation: 11-12 days; female incubates

Fledging: 10-11 days; female and male feed young

Migration: non-migrator in Florida

Food: insects

Compare: Found in a similar habitat as the American Goldfinch (pg. 323), but lacks the male's black forehead and wings. Yellow-rumped Warbler (pg. 211) has only spots of yellow compared with the bright yellow breast of the Common Yellowthroat.

Stan's Notes: A common warbler of open fields and marshes. Has a cheerful, well-known song, "witchity-witchity-witchity-witchity." The male performs a curious courtship display, bouncing in and out of tall grass while uttering an unusual song. The young remain dependent upon the parents longer than most warblers. A frequent cowbird host.

Palm Warbler
Dendroica palmarum

WINTER

Size: 5½" (14 cm)

Male: Distinctive yellow eyebrows. Yellow throat, belly and undertail. Obvious chestnut cap. Thin chestnut streaks on the sides of breast. Dark line across dark eyes.

Female: same as male

Juvenile: same as adult, but duller and brown

Nest: cup; female builds; 1-2 broods per year

Eggs: 4-5; white with brown markings

Incubation: 11-12 days; female incubates

Fledging: 12-13 days; female and male feed young

Migration: complete, to Florida, the West Indies and Central America

Food: insects, fruit

Compare: The Yellow-rumped Warbler (pg. 211) has a similar size, but lacks the yellow throat and belly of the Palm Warbler. Look for the yellow eyebrows and chestnut cap of the Palm Warbler.

Stan's Notes: One of the most common and abundant warblers in Florida during winter, the more common being the Yellow-rumped Warbler. Often seen in backyard woodlands during winter. Look for it to wag or bob its tail while gleaning insects from leaves and flowers of trees. One of the few warblers to feed on the ground. Hops rather than walks. Nests at edges of northern spruce bogs. Recognizes and destroys cowbird eggs, burying them with its nest, which it builds on top of the cowbird nest.

male pg. 285

female

Baltimore Oriole
Icterus galbula

MIGRATION
WINTER

Size: 7-8" (18-20 cm)

Female: A pale yellow bird with orange tones, gray brown wings, white wing bars, a gray bill and dark eyes.

Male: bright flaming orange bird with black head and black extending down nape of neck onto the back, black wings with white and orange wing bars, an orange tail with black streaks, gray bill and dark eyes

Juvenile: same as female

Nest: pendulous; female builds; 1 brood per year

Eggs: 4-5; bluish with brown markings

Incubation: 12-14 days; female incubates

Fledging: 12-14 days; female and male feed young

Migration: complete, to Florida, Mexico, Central and South America

Food: insects, fruit, nectar; comes to orange half and nectar feeders

Compare: Very similar to the female Orchard Oriole (pg. 331), which lacks orange tones and has less pronounced wing bars.

Stan's Notes: A fantastic songster, this bird is often heard before seen. Easily attracted to a feeder offering grape jelly, orange halves or sugar water (nectar). Parents bring young to feeders. Sits in tops of trees feeding on caterpillars. Female builds a sock-like nest at the outermost branches of tall trees. Often returns to the same area year after year. Usually seen during migration and winter.

 CD 2, TRACK 59

male pg. 287

female

Orchard Oriole
Icterus spurius

SUMMER

Size: 7-8" (18-20 cm)

Female: An olive green bird with a dull yellow belly. Has 2 white wing bars on dark gray wings. Long, thin black bill with a small gray mark on lower mandible (jaw).

Male: dull orange with a black head, chin, upper back, wings and tail, single white wing bars

Juvenile: same as female, black bib on first-year male

Nest: pendulous; female builds; 1 brood per year

Eggs: 3-5; pale blue to white, brown markings

Incubation: 11-12 days; female and male incubate

Fledging: 11-14 days; female and male feed young

Migration: complete, to Mexico, Central America and northern South America

Food: insects, fruit; comes to fruit/nectar feeders

Compare: Female Baltimore Oriole (pg. 329) is similar, but has orange tones and more distinct wing bars. Female Summer Tanager (pg. 333) is mustard yellow with a larger bill.

Stan's Notes: Prefers orchards or open woods, hence its common name. Eats insects until wild fruit starts to ripen. Summer resident in the northern part of Florida. Often nests alone, but sometimes nests in small colonies. Parents bring young to jelly and orange half feeders just after fledging. Many think the orioles have left during the summer, but the birds are concentrating on finding insects to feed their young.

 CD 2, TRACK 60

male pg. 293

female

YEAR-ROUND
SUMMER
WINTER

Summer Tanager
Piranga rubra

Size: 8" (20 cm)

Female: Some show a faint wash of red, but most females are a mustard yellow overall with slightly darker wings.

Male: bright rosy red bird with darker red wings

Juvenile: male has patches of red and green over the entire body, female is same as adult female

Nest: cup; female builds; 1-2 broods per year

Eggs: 3-5; pale blue with dark markings

Incubation: 10-12 days; female incubates

Fledging: unknown days; female and male feed young

Migration: complete, to Florida, Central America and South America

Food: insects, fruit

Compare: Similar to female Orchard Oriole (pg. 331) and Baltimore Oriole (pg. 329), but female Summer Tanager lacks wing bars and has a larger, thicker bill.

Stan's Notes: A distinctive bird of woodlands in Florida, especially in mixed pine and oak forests. Due to the clearing of land for agriculture, populations have decreased over the past 100 years and especially in the last 20 years. Returning to Florida in late March and with young hatching in May, some pairs have two broods per year. Most leave the state by November with very few remaining for winter. While fruit makes up some of the diet, most of it consists of insects such as bees and wasps. Summer Tanagers unfortunately seem to be parasitized by Brown-headed Cowbirds more than just about any other nesting bird in Florida.

YEAR-ROUND

Eastern Meadowlark
Sturnella magna

Size: 9" (22.5 cm)

Male: Robin-shaped bird with a yellow breast and belly, brown back and prominent black V-shaped necklace. White outer tail feathers.

Female: same as male

Juvenile: same as adult

Nest: cup, on the ground in dense cover; female builds; 2 broods per year

Eggs: 3-5; white with brown markings

Incubation: 13-15 days; female incubates

Fledging: 11-12 days; female and male feed young

Migration: non-migrator in Florida

Food: insects, seeds

Compare: This is the only large yellow bird that has a black V mark on the breast.

Stan's Notes: A bird of open grassy country. Named "Meadowlark" because it's a bird of meadows and sings like the larks of Europe. Best known for its wonderful song—a flute-like, clear whistle. Often seen perching on fence posts, it will quickly dive into tall grass if approached. Conspicuous white markings on each side of its tail, most often seen when flying away. Nest is sometimes domed with dried grass. Not a member of the lark family, it actually belongs to the blackbird family and is related to grackles and orioles.

 CD 2, TRACK 77

HELPFUL RESOURCES

Birder's Bug Book, The. Waldbauer, Gilbert. Cambridge: Harvard University Press, 1998.

Birder's Dictionary. Cox, Randall T. Helena, MT: Falcon Press Publishing, 1996.

Birder's Handbook, The. Ehrlich, Paul R., David S. Dobkin and Darryl Wheye. New York: Simon and Schuster, 1988.

Birds Do It, Too: The Amazing Sex Life of Birds. Harrison, Kit and George H. Harrison. Minocqua, WI: Willow Creek Press, 1997.

Birds of Forest, Yard, and Thicket. Eastman, John. Mechanicsburg, PA: Stackpole Books, 1997.

Birds of North America. Kaufman, Kenn. New York: Houghton Mifflin, 2000.

Blackbirds of the Americas. Orians, Gordon H. Seattle: University of Washington Press, 1985.

Cardinal, The. Osborne, June. Austin: University of Texas Press, 1995.

Cry of the Sandhill Crane, The. Grooms, Steve. Minocqua, WI: NorthWord Press, 1992.

Dictionary of American Bird Names, The. Choate, Ernest A. Boston: Harvard Common Press, 1985.

Dictionary of Birds of the United States. Holloway, Joel E. Portland, OR: Timber Press, 2003.

Everything You Never Learned About Birds. Rupp, Rebecca. Pownal, VT: Storey Publishing, 1997.

Field Guide to the Birds, A: A Completely New Guide to All the Birds of Eastern and Central North America. Peterson, Roger Tory and Virginia Marie Peterson. Boston: Houghton Mifflin, 1998.

Field Guide to the Birds of North America: Third Edition. Washington, DC: National Geographic Society, 1999.

Field Guide to Warblers of North America, A. Dunn, Jon and Kimball Garrett. Boston: Houghton Mifflin, 1997.

Florida's Birds: A Handbook and Reference. Kale, Herbert, W., II and David S. Maehr. Sarasota: Pineapple Press, 1990.

Florida Birds Species: An Annotated List, Special Publication No. 6. Robertson, William B., Jr. and Glen E. Woolfenden. n.p.: Florida Ornithological Society, 1992.

Folklore of Birds. Martin, Laura C. Old Saybrook, CT: Globe Pequot Press, 1996.

Guide to Bird Behavior, A: Vol I, II, III. Stokes, Donald and Lillian Stokes. Boston: Little, Brown and Company, 1989.

How Birds Migrate. Kerlinger, Paul. Mechanicsburg, PA: Stackpole Books, 1995.

Lives of Birds, The: Birds of the World and Their Behavior. Short, Lester L. Collingdale, PA: DIANE Publishing, 2000.

Living on the Wind. Weidensaul, Scott. New York: North Point Press, 2000.

National Audubon Society: North American Birdfeeder Handbook. Burton, Robert. New York: Dorling Kindersley Publishing, 1995.

National Audubon Society: The Sibley Guide to Bird Life and Behavior. Edited by David Allen Sibley, Chris Elphick and John B. Dunning, Jr. New York: Alfred A. Knopf, 2001.

National Audubon Society: The Sibley Guide to Birds. Sibley, David Allen. New York: Alfred A. Knopf, 2000.

Photographic Guide to North American Raptors, A. Wheeler, Brian K. and William S. Clark. New York: Academic Press, 1999.

Raptors of Eastern North America: The Wheeler Guides. Wheeler, Brian K. Princeton, NJ: Princeton University Press, 2003.

Secret Lives of Birds, The. Gingras, Pierre. Toronto: Key Porter Books, 1997.

Secrets of the Nest. Dunning, Joan. Boston: Houghton Mifflin, 1994.

Sparrows and Buntings: A Guide to the Sparrows and Buntings of North America and the World. Byers, Clive, Jon Curson and Urban Olsson. New York: Houghton Mifflin, 1995.

Stokes Bluebird Book: The Complete Guide to Attracting Bluebirds. Stokes, Donald and Lillian Stokes. Boston: Little, Brown and Company, 1991.

Stokes Field Guide to Birds: Eastern Region. Stokes, Donald and Lillian Stokes. Boston: Little, Brown and Company, 1996.

Stokes Purple Martin Book. Stokes, Donald and Lillian Stokes. Boston: Little, Brown and Company, 1997.

Florida Birding Hotlines

To report unusual bird sightings or possibly hear recordings of where birds have been seen, you can often call pre-recorded hotlines detailing such information. Since these hotlines are usually staffed by volunteers, and phone numbers and even the organizations that host them often change, the phone numbers are not listed here. To obtain the numbers, go to your favorite internet search engine, type in something like "rare bird alert hotline Florida" and follow the links provided.

Web Pages

The internet is a valuable place to learn more about birds. You may find birding on the net a fun way to discover additional information or to spend a long winter night. These web sites will assist you in your pursuit of birds. If a web address doesn't work (they often change a bit), just enter the name of the group into a search engine to track down the new web address.

Site	Address
Audubon of Florida	www.audubonofflorida.org
Tropical Audubon Society	www.tropicalaudubon.org
Florida Ornithological Society	www.fosbirds.org
American Birding Association	www.americanbirding.org
Cornell Lab of Ornithology	www.birds.cornell.edu
Author Stan Tekiela's home page	www.naturesmart.com

CHECK LIST/INDEX BY SPECIES

Use the boxes to check the birds you've seen.

"CD Track" refers to the *Birds of Florida Audio CDs* by Stan Tekiela.

"CD Track" refers to the *Birds of Florida Audio CDs* by Stan Tekiela.

"CD Track" refers to the *Birds of Florida Audio CDs* by Stan Tekiela.

"CD Track" refers to the *Birds of Florida Audio CDs* by Stan Tekiela.

"CD Track" refers to the *Birds of Florida Audio CDs* by Stan Tekiela.

"CD Track" refers to the *Birds of Florida Audio CDs* by Stan Tekiela.

ABOUT THE AUTHOR

Stan Tekiela is a naturalist, author and wildlife photographer with a Bachelor of Science degree in Natural History from the University of Minnesota. He has been a professional naturalist for more than 20 years and is a member of the Minnesota Naturalist Association, Minnesota Ornithologist Union, Outdoor Writers Association of America, North American Nature Photography Association and Canon Professional Services. Stan actively studies and photographs birds throughout the United States. He has received various national and regional awards for outdoor education and writing. A columnist and radio personality, his syndicated column appears in over 20 cities and he can be heard on a number of radio stations. Stan resides in Victoria, Minnesota, with wife Katherine and daughter Abigail. He can be contacted via his web page at www.naturesmart.com.

Stan authors field guides for other states including guides for birds, birds of prey, mammals, reptiles and amphibians, trees and wildflowers.